Is Reincarnation an Illusion?

This book looks at reincarnation from many different perspectives to test whether this is really a very complex illusion.

Geoff Cutler
July, 2016 (Revision 1)

Is Reincarnation an Illusion?

Copyright © 2016 by Geoffrey John Cutler. Copyright is claimed by the author in this work. All rights are reserved. No part of this book may be reproduced or transmitted in any form or by any means, electronic or mechanical, including photocopying, recording or by any information storage and retrieval system without permission in writing from the author.

The author also acknowledges the inclusion of material from other sources, both currently copyrighted, that with an expired copyright, and that in the public domain. Chapter 16 of this book is based on another publication by the author, "Getting the Hell Out of Here" which has previously been provided free of charge in electronic format.

Where extensive quotes have been used from works still covered by copyright, permission has been granted by the publisher. The author acknowledges the permission received from Hickman Healing Foundation, and Dr Stanislov Grof. Actually all sources quoted, where an existing publisher could be found, were approached for permission. Most would not reply to emails, and it has been assumed are completely disinterested in the matter of attributed quotations.

This first revision has some additional material that came to light after initial publication in 2011. This is in chapters 1 and 7.

July 2016, Bayview, NSW, Australia.
Author: Geoffrey John Cutler.

ISBN: 978-1-4477-8050-2

The front and back cover design is by Lulu.

Is Reincarnation an illusion?

Preface.

I decided to write this book to summarise all the issues regarding reincarnation, after about ten years of looking at it both as a believer, and ultimately as a non-believer. I will admit upfront that I do not believe in reincarnation – not anymore. But it is also clear that you cannot glibly dismiss the claims of those who do believe in reincarnation. It would not surprise me to find that over half the people alive today believe in reincarnation; in fact one of my favourite books says three quarters. And, amongst many seekers of truth in the Western world – the so called "new age" – this belief is very common. In fact it's so endemic, that when you question folks on it, they may say that it's indisputable. And, as we will see later, there is some good evidence why many would take that line.

But let's start with a definition of reincarnation that will not satisfy everyone, but is what I am taking for the purposes of this book:

> The belief that a human soul must return **repeatedly** to **this planet** in order to experience lessons and to grow spiritually, until finally a sufficient level of spirituality is achieved to terminate this cycle.

While there are many variations, typically this Earth is the only place that spiritual lessons are learned, and karma expiated, and little or no focus is put on that final exit stage, all the interest being on this life, and what went before. There is however at least one popular practitioner that I know of interested in the future as well as the now – Brian Weiss[1]. To be honest, some in Asia tend to view the objective of life as

---

[1] *Same Soul, Many Bodies* by Brian L. Weiss, M.D. published by Free Press, ISBN 0-7432-6433-9

not reincarnating – avoiding another cycle - and so that is again a slightly different view.

There are plenty of variations on this concept of reincarnation, which is why I will stick to this definition. Accordingly talking about spiritual progression and learning lessons **in the next realm**, does not form a part of this definition, and is not considered by me to be any part of reincarnation.

It should be noted that for most people, a belief in reincarnation or a disbelief in that philosophy probably has no spiritual effect. By that I mean it is not inherently dangerous, or negative or spiritually damaging. What I am alluding to here is that, as far as I can determine, what happens to you after death is not primarily a function of what you believe. I say most people, because I have found some pernicious beliefs amongst some folk.

I have found some who believe that evil is an important part of our path, and that those who are evil, should be applauded for giving the rest of us our growth opportunities. It is, in my view, very dangerous to consider that evil is in fact, "good". It is true that experiencing evil can sometimes lead to positive outcomes, but that does not make evil a good thing. Many of course do believe that for good to exist, evil must also exist. This is part of a classic belief in the duality of all things. But love does not have a dual. Moving from infinite love to the absence of love is not a duality, merely a variation in volume. Hate is not the opposite of love. You can have love, and the absence of love. Hate emanates from fear, and is a very different issue. Many things do appear to have duals, but it is, in my opinion, not a universal phenomenon. Those that believe in duality, then naturally consider that God must be capable of evil. This I do not believe. Evil is the result of incorrect choices, choices that conflict with God's Will. Evil exists only because we have free will. But one thing that I do believe is that our choices have outcomes, or karma in reincarnation-speak. Both positive and negative outcomes.

Of course there are a number of things that we notice about life that have not generally been satisfactorily explained by most religions – those that do not subscribe to reincarnation anyway. Take for example the issue of a still born child, or a child lost in its infancy. If you consider that our purpose here is to grow and learn, clearly that has not been achieved. Proceeding further along this line of thought, what about those who carry physical defects through life. Maybe they are mentally disabled, or hugely physically disabled? Considering that you will get another chance does seem the sort of thing a loving God would arrange. In my personal search for Truth, I have found an answer to this particular puzzle that does not involve reincarnation.

Provided you do the best you can in this life, it makes no difference to your spiritual progress achieved here whether you will return in the flesh, or not. So, in some respects, you could say: "Who cares?"

Unfortunately folks do care. This topic is a real switch-off. What I mean by that, is if you are a believer in reincarnation, and you come across a group of folk who believe otherwise, or a book, the chances are you will pass on. And the reverse is equally true. This is sad really, because as I have discovered, folks of both persuasions have Truth to share. In fact quite specifically two books I will refer to in this book, *"Letters from a living dead man"*[2] and *"The Urantia Book"*[3] actually corroborate each other in at least two places on esoteric topics that I have had great difficulty verifying.

But these two books are on opposite sides of the reincarnation debate. And if you only read one of them, you would be the loser. Indeed it was not long ago that I had that view myself. I gave up on Neale Donald Walsch (author of "Conversations with God") because his "god" believes in reincarnation. While I am not sure that I am about to rush out and buy his complete series, I am these days open to reading any book that comes highly recommended, even if it favours the reincarnation angle. And that includes recommendations from strangers. Indeed it was on personal recommendations that I bought *"Letters from a living dead man"*, *"Remote Depossession"*[4] and *"Life on the Other Side."*[5] That last book I bought because someone said a booklet[6] I had written was very similar to Sylvia Browne's book, so I

---

[2] *"Letters from a living dead man"* as written through the hand of Elsa Barker, originally published in London by W. Rider, 1914 re-published by Beyond Words Publishing in 1995 as *"Letters from the Light"*, ISBN 1-885223-08-0

[3] *"The Urantia Book"*, published by Urantia Foundation, 1955. ISBN 0-911560-51-3

[4] *"Remote Depossession"* by Dr Irene Hickman, published by Hickman Systems 1994, ISBN 09156898-08-1

[5] *"Life on The Other Side"*, by Sylvia Browne, published by Judy Piatkus (Publishers) Limited in 2000. ISBN 0-7499-2182-X

[6] This is included in this publication as Chapter 16.

thought I better have a look at it. All three of these books have contributed significantly to my discourse here.

I do not claim that this book is based on scientific principles of research – repeatability or even probability. My interest extends primarily to communications with discarnates – spirits and angels. These are impossible subjects for scientific evaluation, even though science is just beginning to prove that this sort of thing looks possible, it will probably never be possible to verify a specific communication scientifically. It's a bit like science agreeing telephony works, and accurately connects two parties, but cannot judge whether what those parties have to say, on a given day, is accurate or not.

Nevertheless I do use my own approach in an attempt to weed through the vast numbers of spirit communications that are out there, and find sources that appear to be reasonably accurate. The issue of spirit communication and accuracy is relevant, and complex. One cannot assume any communication is inherently accurate, based on the receiver, the source, or the fact that previous communications have appeared sound. Good receivers have bad days; most receivers have a belief system that all too easily gets directly in the way, and taints the message. For a starter I rely on what I call the Spirit of Truth that really means that I find the message resonates with Truth for me. This sadly must be a subjective process, although I confess that I can't see that it should be. But personal experience has shown me that it often is, when you find two folks both claiming the Spirit of Truth, yet holding opposite views. After that, I like to find a second source that has much the same thing. More is better, but something completely left wing requires at least two different sources for my complete satisfaction.

I initially made the assumption that those who believe in reincarnation would also be likely to be open to spirit communication. This seems logical to me, but has not proved to be true. If you are not willing to accept that spirits can communicate from across the divide, then this book will probably not be attractive to you. Because almost without exception the books or references quoted here concern communications that have been received from the "other side." I think many of those who believe in reincarnation yet do not believe in spirit communication may have been influenced by Madame Blavatsky the founder of Theosophy. I understand that while here she strongly discouraged spirit communication. The Urantia Foundation takes a similar view, even as it claims its book came from supernatural sources.

Is there any chance that this book might cause someone to change their views? Well not without a lot of intellectual stress. I know that, having traveled that road. I think giving up on the idea of reincarnation was harder for me to accept than recognizing that Jesus is not the Prime Source, nor any part of it. Both caused a great deal of internal anguish. But to be spiritually fearless you must be prepared to destroy long cherished beliefs. I guess the best I might hope for is a re-assessment of the reasons why folks believe in reincarnation, or an openness where previously they might have been "certain". Perhaps they might also read some of the books I have quoted here, and with the benefit of having read the whole book, be able to form a better opinion of the matter. Even if at the end, they can simply say: "Who cares," I think we will have moved forward.

Geoff Cutler.
Bayview, NSW, Australia.
First Revision July 2016.

Table of Contents

Chapter 1 Eastern beliefs. 3
Chapter 2 The Bible. 19
Chapter 3 Where is the mind? 25
Chapter 4 Past Life Memories. 29
Chapter 5 "Past Life" researcher Ian Stevenson. 41
Chapter 6 The Law of Attraction. 55
Chapter 7 Trying to Reincarnate. 61
Chapter 8 The soul and the spirit body. 107
Chapter 9 Sleeping Survivors. 113
Chapter 10 Non-survivors of death. 125
Chapter 11 Hell. 127
Chapter 12 Getting out of Hell. 139
Chapter 13 Progress in spirit. 151
Chapter 14 Hearing from famous spirits. 161
Chapter 15 Indwelling Spirits – the perfect Guide. 165
Chapter 16 What really happens after death? 169
    Death. 169
    The Structure of the Heavens. 176
    The Astral Plane. 181
    Hell. 184
    The First Sphere. 191
    The Second Sphere. 194

The Third Sphere... 196
The Fourth Sphere. 198
The Fifth Sphere.. 199
The Sixth Sphere... 201
The Seventh Sphere.. 203
Recommended reading:..*205*

Is Reincarnation an illusion?

Chapter 1

Eastern beliefs.

Eastern religions, particularly Buddhists and the Hindu in India have long supported a belief in reincarnation, but this also extends to many other religions in that part of the world as well. Many, who follow this belief, particularly in India, seem to me to be very fatalistic about life. It is very much a case of, well it's tough now, but it will be better next time round. Or alternatively – it's tough now, because I was silly last time round. That may well be a good coping mechanism for a difficult life on a material level, but I hope it does not have the same effect on their spiritual practices. In other words, I rather hope they give due attention to their spiritual practices right now, no matter what their material circumstances. But from the little I know about them, large numbers of them seem to be really devout. In fact, if anything, they may well be more spiritually oriented than the western societies dominated by Christian beliefs. Maybe a belief that you personally will pay for what you do is more effective in building loving societies? Certainly India in recent history can show the rest of the world the only non-violent "civil uprising" ever not fought. And our Western societies such as the USA and UK cannot demonstrate anything like that, in terms of non-aggression. Of course it could simply be the lack of rampant materialism in India that has kept them more spiritual?

There are also subtle differences in the perspective on reincarnation that one can observe amongst "new age" Westerners, and those in the East. The new age folks do seem very keen to reincarnate here, whereas the Easterners are truly not at all keen to reincarnate, they want the cycle to end.

Is Reincarnation an Illusion?

Why do the Eastern religions believe in reincarnation? Well, amongst the Buddhist there are some astonishing stories of the search for the next Dalai Lama. Are these made up? I doubt that very much. Indeed I am pretty sure they are correct. Once the Dalai Lama passes on, a search begins for the next. This involves monks reviewing children who appear to have some potential, according to certain signs that the monks are looking for. Eventually they typically find a young child who displays an amazing awareness of the previous Dalai Lama. Is this not proof of past lives?

I have pondered on this very subject a long time. More particularly, the case of Sai Baba in India has intrigued me. Here was/is an extremely spiritually advanced individual, who not only believes he is the reincarnation of another, but has stated when precisely he will reincarnate. Then one day I picked up the Urantia book, and opened it, and a passage caught my eye. It was talking about Thought Adjusters, and Mystery Monitors. I personally dislike the terms that the Urantia Book uses, in particular the term "Thought Adjuster", and in this book I will mostly use the term Indwelling Spirit, but of course quotes from the Urantia Book will refer to Thought Adjusters.

I will now have to introduce a topic that you very likely have never heard of, or if you have heard of it, it may be in terms of some sort of vague "Higher Consciousness". Perhaps I might start with a little background on what an Indwelling Spirit is, taken from The Urantia Book:

> *Although the Universal Father is personally resident on Paradise, at the very center of the universes, he is also actually present on the worlds of space in the minds of his countless children of time, for he indwells them as the Mystery Monitors. The eternal Father is at one and the same time farthest removed from, and most intimately associated with, his planetary mortal sons.*[7]

and

> *Though there are diverse opinions regarding the mode of the bestowal of Thought Adjusters, there exist no*

---
[7] *The Urantia Book*, page 1176.

> such differences concerning their origin; all are agreed that they proceed direct from the Universal Father, the First Source and Center. They are not created beings; they are fragmentized entities constituting the factual presence of the infinite God. Together with their many unrevealed associates, the Adjusters are undiluted and unmixed divinity, unqualified and unattenuated parts of Deity; they are of God, and as far as we are able to discern, **they are God.**[8]

and

> No matter what the previous status of the inhabitants of a world, subsequent to the bestowal of a divine Son and after the bestowal of the Spirit of Truth upon all humans, the Adjusters flock to such a world to indwell the minds of all normal will creatures. Following the completion of the mission of a Paradise bestowal Son, these Monitors truly become the "kingdom of heaven within you."[9]

The only place I have ever found this concept discussed is in the Urantia book, other than passing and often vague references in other places, and a number of unpublished communications that a friend of mine received, but usually these sources do not make any attempt at an explanation as to what really constitutes an inner voice, also called a pilot light, or even a higher consciousness.

Now you may choose to simply dismiss this as yet another strange belief system, although there are today a surprising number of people who will tell you they do converse with their Indwelling Spirit, and I would include myself amongst those. I will present many other concepts along the way, hoping to produce substantial numbers of things that all seem to point against reincarnation being true. If you choose to dismiss everything in this book as a belief system, then you might realize that your own foundation is probably based on "belief." I am not philosophically opposed to that, but my own approach is to read anything, no matter whether it is meant to be a belief, a channeled source, or scientific research. For sure I dismiss things, but not

---

[8] *The Urantia Book,* page 1177.
[9] *The Urantia Book,* page 1193.

Is Reincarnation an Illusion?

generally simply because they are part of someone's "belief system." By the very nature of things, discussions about the other side and communications with the other side are tenuous, and can be dismissed if one is of a mind to do so.

Here is the quote from The Urantia Book referring to transfer of "past life" information between two individuals which triggered my interest:

> The reservists unconsciously act as conservators of essential planetary information. Many times, upon the death of a reservist, a transfer of certain vital data from the mind of the dying reservist to a younger successor is made by a liason of the two Thought Adjusters. The Adjusters undoubtedly function in many other ways unknown to us, in connection with these reserve corps[10].

I have a circle of friends who are able to receive messages from spirit. We have actually asked those spirit beings with whom we are in contact, whether this particular passage explains the past life memories of individuals like the Dalai Lama and Sai Baba, and had it confirmed in the case of the former. No initial comment was forthcoming regarding Sai Baba. One of these communications is quoted on page 13.

The Urantia Book tells that after Jesus' sojourn here, we mortals were universally granted the great privilege to be indwelt by a Divine Fragment – an Indwelling Spirit. This is referred to in an earlier quote as: *"subsequent to the bestowal of a divine Son and after the bestowal of the Spirit of Truth upon all humans."* This Indwelling Spirit "resides" in a part of our upper mind, hence the name "Indwelling Spirit." It is in fact capable of departing, and may do so, generally when we are asleep. This entity is apparently absolutely Divine, and eternal. It has enormous knowledge, and is in every respect, a fragment of God. Its role is to lead us to make the right decisions in our lives, and it has access to "the future". If we follow its leading, ultimately we will be sufficiently spiritually advanced to be capable of fusion with this divine entity, thereby transforming ourselves into an eternal divine being. It is possible to develop one's mind to the point where dialogue with this

---

[10] *The Urantia Book*, page 1258.

Eastern Beliefs.

entity is possible. Indeed quite a number of folks have achieved that. This is literally "the kingdom within."

Why would the Indwelling Spirit allow this, or even be interested in this? Apparently it has no personality, although we would find it hard to understand how anything could exist devoid of personality, never mind a Divine being. So the quid pro quo is that it gains personality, and you gain the eternal status of a Divine being – immortality, access to amazing knowledge, etc. But this fused status is only reached with the full commitment of the mortal, and some mortals apparently choose not to follow this path. This then results in Indwelling Spirits who do indeed have a second shot at guiding another mortal. One might in passing wonder why a Fragment of God, with access to the future, would indwell a being that is going to refuse to fuse, but in fact that experience is useful, and utilized.

Some non-Christians may be upset by this concept of Indwelling Spirits, because there is an apparent link to Jesus as having had some role in their presence here, but it's not something any orthodox Christian Church teaches. While Indwelling Spirits were apparently not universally available before Jesus' sojourn here, they were provided to those individuals who were of a high spiritual outlook. There would be little doubt that the Buddha, as an example, could have gained a Indwelling Spirit, but whether he did so would probably have been influenced by his apparent disinterest in the concept of God.

So the concept is not necessarily a "Christian" concept, although it is asserted in The Urantia Book that Jesus played a critical role in their becoming universally available. Not simply to "Christians" however, but to all mortals. And it is certainly not a concept that can be found in the Christian Bible, except in as much as Jesus frequently refers to the Kingdom as being "within" and of course the reference to being reborn of spirit in order to enter the Kingdom of God refers to reaching a state of fusion with this divine entity.

But to return to the Dalai Lama. So how does this Indwelling Spirit play a role in the case of the Dalai Lama? A very small number of individuals are classified as being of significant spiritual heritage to this world, and their Indwelling Spirits play a role in maintaining this spiritual heritage. The entire experience and life details can be transferred by one Indwelling Spirit to another Indwelling Spirit, and thus become available in the mind of the next human who is known to the Divine to be the next Dalai Lama. This store of passed on spiritual and other knowledge then seals the deal, as it were, to the human seekers of the next incumbent. This situation however only pertains to a very small number of individuals, maybe no more than a thousand, possibly even as few as a hundred. Of course these individuals are high profile in their religious societies, and having a good access to the knowledge placed in their minds by their Indwelling Spirit; it is not surprising that a belief in past lives would become firmly established. One could argue that it is absolutely true for them because the information was placed in their minds – their local mind.

But to return to Sai Baba; for information I am forced to rely on books that others have written to learn about this individual, and I do take these as pretty accurate, but of course I can't be sure. Sadly he has now passed over, leaving even more questions unanswered. A book that I came by recently: "Sai Baba. The Holy Man..... And the Psychiatrist."[11] once again triggered my interest in this enigmatic personality. Reading the book closely, I gathered that he claimed to be an Avatar, a descender from Paradise, and "Lord of Lords" – literally God manifest on Earth. I was discussing this with a particularly gifted psychic friend, when he said just one word: "**Transcendentaler**". In other words, it appeared that spirit had just passed on that information to him. Now a Transcendental being is indeed a Paradise resident group of extremely advanced entities. You could look that up in the Urantia Book in paper 30:

> ***EVENTUATED TRANSCENDENTAL BEINGS.*** *There is to be found on Paradise a vast host of transcendental beings whose origin is not ordinarily disclosed to the universes of time and space until they are settled in light and life. These Transcendentalers are neither creators nor creatures; they are the eventuated children of divinity, ultimacy, and eternity. These "eventuators" are neither finite nor infinite--they are absonite; and absonity is neither infinity nor absoluteness.*[12]

---

[11] *Sai Baba. The Holy Man.......And The Psychiatrist.* By Samuel H. Sandweiss, M.D. ISBN 0-9600958-1-0

[12] *The Urantia Book*, paper 30

Eastern Beliefs.

As of 2011 I had accepted that to be true and that Sai Baba was the most advanced being I personally knew of on this planet. (He passed over on the 24th April 2011.) If that is true, there is indeed no reason why he should not return again as a teacher. And it's certainly not for me to say whether he should or will. But that process is not what I call reincarnation. Because if he is not the same as us, and he is not returning to advance spiritually, then it's not reincarnation in the simple sense. Did he teach reincarnation? Well if he did, it did not seem to be a central feature of that book. He seemed to be a lot more focused on the need to connect with God, at a personal level, through love. That is as far as I can go. But this last mentioned book certainly contains a tale that does suggest he is supportive of that concept. But would it be otherwise? Would this teacher have over a million followers if he announced that reincarnation is false? I wonder. But what I did not know, is what his views were on **our** paths, the paths of ordinary ascending mortals. But this tale from this book concerns a Walter Cowan, allegedly brought back from the dead on Christmas Day in 1971 by Sai Baba. This is related on page 101 of the quoted book. This extract below is similar but is not in fact from that book, but from yet another book by John Hislop: "My Baba and I":

> *Walter described his experience. He said he realized that he had died and that he had remained with the body, in the ambulance, looking at it with interest. Then Baba came and together they went to a place, which seemed to be at a great height. There they entered a conference room where people were seated around a table. There was a presiding chairman who had a kind face and who spoke in a kindly way. He called for Walter's records and these were read aloud. The records were in different languages and Walter did not understand what was said until after some time when Baba started to translate. Walter was surprised to hear that he had occupied a lofty status in various times and cultures and had always been dedicated to the welfare of the people. At length, Baba addressed the person presiding and asked that Walter be given over to Baba's care, for Baba had work for Walter to do. Then, when Baba and he departed the room, Walter felt himself descending towards a place where his body was, but felt great reluctance. In terms of direct experience, he had realized that he was not the body, and*

Is Reincarnation an Illusion?

> *he had no wish to be subject again to anxieties and miseries.*[13]

Now this appears to indicate that Sai Baba participated in some sort of life review that encompassed more than one life. I have to confess that I cannot explain this; it is contrary to all that I know of what happens after death. It would also suggest that Sai Baba believes that we mortals reincarnate. I subsequently purchased a copy of "My Baba and I" and learned from it that John Hislop was believed to have spent more time with Sai Baba than any other Westerner. Accordingly, one could place some reliance on the discussion of his teachings in this book, and probably draw reasonable conclusions. It is clear from his book, that Sai Baba did support reincarnation, although once again one is left with the feeling that his emphasis was on transcending rebirth, and much more focussed on achieving union with God. But, Sai Baba has recently passed over, and even that event has raised yet more questions. He predicted he would die at 96, yet he did not, passing at 85. He also fell ill at the end, and was hospitalised for a month, in spite of being such a powerful healer of others. These are not minor issues if you claim to be God on Earth. However we suddenly received a communication in 2014 regarding Sai Baba and I have to say it rather surprised me. It surprised me because it directly contradicts what I quoted above about Sai Baba being a transcendentaler, it indicated the sphere into which he passed, and tells of the gifts he displayed while here and which were often disputed as magic tricks. Here is that message:

> *February 4th, 2014*
> *Frankfurt.*
> *Received by WV.*
>
> *I am here, your friend and helper, Sri Yukteswar. (He was Yogananda's guru.)*
> *I have come because I wanted to reply to the question who Sai Baba was.*
> *Well let me start off with saying he wasn't an avatar. When he died he entered what is known as the fourth sphere. He was not more special than any other man on earth. He was born from a woman and he died as any other man will have to, once.*

---

[13] *"My Baba and I"* by John Hislop

The reason why he was able to do some things others can't is he understood the Laws of Creation. These laws govern the way things are created and also how they are destroyed. When you come to learn how your free will can interact with these laws, you will understand the way they work.

Sai Baba wasn't any different except that he knew how to interact with the Laws of Creation. It is because of this he could create or manifest things other people can't. I have known many people who understood the Laws of Creation and could do the things Sai Baba could. So you see he wasn't further advanced than any other human could be.

The problem with most humans is they don't believe it is possible to create things out of nothing or thin air. But if you look closely at how Mother Nature works, you will find she does it all the time. The only things she needs are the right conditions to do so, and off she goes to create what is needed to be.

So the fast learner, or at least the attentive one, will understand the last sentence is the key to the whole mystery: "creating the right conditions". How? Well, everything created is done so with "intention". So you see these three things are very important when it comes to materializing or dematerializing things: "free will, intention and the right conditions." The third parameter is actually influenced or created by the help of the first two.

I know this all sounds a bit confusing at first but when you meditate upon this for a little while, it will become very clear to you. But, to confuse you even more, I have to say these parameters are all influenced by your mind and mental beliefs. These parameters all have their origin in the soul. So if you do not let the soul supersede the mind, you will never be able to materialize or dematerialize.

I am going to stop here for now and hope you find interest in what I have given you. Keep an open mind so we can pour our knowledge into your consciousness, my dear friend.

Goodbye, your friend and helper, Sri Yukteswar.

Is Reincarnation an Illusion?

Now I know this medium VW well, and have great confidence in him and the spirit is certainly competent enough and advanced enough to know. The matter of his passing into the Fourth Sphere is impressive compared with the average of humanity, but it is a very long way from a "divine being". It is however surprising to me for another reason but I can't discuss this now; it will be much clearer later in chapter 16 when the differences in the spheres are discussed. But it's interesting to hear that he did indeed have the ability to materialize things. Of course this will be no surprise to his believers, but he had a great number of forthright critics. So that is the end of my discussion on Sai Baba and it ends as a damp squib because it seems he was not who he thought he was – God. So his opinions on other things must be questioned.

We come now to a variation on the scenario which causes one Dalia Lama to obtain past life information from the Indwelling Spirit of the recently deceased previous Dalai Lama. This variation is caused by experienced Indwelling Spirits. A number of folks do have experienced Indwelling Spirits – those who have had a previous mortal charge refuse the fusion option, and who have as a result been allocated to another mortal. These Adjusters do have previous life experiences, and in some cases, this experience may be shared with the mortal charge. This can be yet another source of "past life" experiences, but since all these experiences were on another planet, in at least some cases one would expect that to emerge, if the source is the Indwelling Spirit. I have come across a very small number of folks who claim that they are actually "aliens" reincarnated here. This explanation is a possible reason for them believing that, although my narrow definition of reincarnation would exclude those who come here in an advanced condition to teach. I confess that I do not discount the possibility that there might be some here from another planet as advanced teachers. But I don't count them as "normal" humans for the purposes of this book. But I would also expect some very normal humans, having their first material life experience here, have an Indwelling Spirit with previous life experience on another planet. And some of them will discover that data.

Eastern Beliefs.

Here is an extract of a message from "Andrea", a 500,000 year old primary midwayer,[14] answering the question of where past life memories come from:

> Over the years, much information on the subject has been uploaded into your mind, but it is my pleasure entirely to be speaking about the tenacious, endemic religious belief systems that include reincarnation of many types, and from the very droll to the outright ridiculous.
>
> I guess there is some value in hearing it from me. And even with my lengthy overview of how these experiences and thoughts have become myths and have turned into belief systems that so many of your siblings adhere to, yes, even in the predominantly Christian world, it is not always clearly understood even by the likes of me how these credos have metamorphosed into such a myriad range.
>
> At times, the connection between the experienced Father Fragment and the human deep mind will give rise to 'a knowing' at a conscious level, and herein the truest form of suggestion of reincarnation – and I want you to put these words in quotation marks – may become evident. These are actual experiences in the lifetimes of Father Fragments that served well in the lives of some (humans), who may or may not have proceeded to undertake an eternity existence.
>
> And so it is on your world, our world, our troubled, blighted and chaotic world, that so many highly experienced Fragments of the Creator of All are attracted to serve in the most difficult and yet experientially profitable of circumstances. And it is therefore fair to say that among you there are many who are recollecting meaningful aspects of previous Father Fragment existences that may well come through in an accurate, partly garbled, or even disordered way.

---

[14] (Midwayers are semi-material beings, closely associated with this planet, and intended to be the first Spiritual Teachers for mankind. They are described more fully in The Urantia Book in paper 37 and 77.) http://www.urantia.org/urantia-book-standardized/paper-77-midway-creatures?

Is Reincarnation an Illusion?

> *For the vast majority of you, the difficulty with the interpretation of these 'elements of knowing' lies in the lack of your spiritual and religious understanding of your very make-up; your inability to differentiate between the pre-existent Father Fragment and the newly appointed soul that will carry you to eternal life at the time of your mortal demise.*
>
> *The soul is but a mere seed of future potential in a small child. It is ticket, a tiny IOU, or voucher, one might say, that through the job of living a rightful, righteous, thankful, gracious and spiritual life in its future will grow, develop and mature into a sparkling new you with the potential of eternal service, enjoyment and certainty of your being drawn ever Paradise-ward.*
>
> *Yes, of course, these perhaps accidental communications between the Father Fragment and the deep mind do at times surface. However, in your earnest endeavor of trying to collect information about, and learning from previous soul lives, there is rarely the accuracy one might assign to what can admittedly be so vividly experienced.*
>
> *Each of you have been gifted with mind endowments that will only 'attach and interconnect' with unqualified degrees of fullness and accuracy. Your groupings of interactive mind segments have the ability to reach out at any given time, one might say, to only God knows where, and acknowledge the information gained as belonging to your soul's pasts, when there are no such pasts.*
>
> *All kinds of details are available, and from myriad sources, and even from our enhanced view, and with our lengthy experience, we cannot always fathom from where these seemingly accurate details of previous soul lives may have been gathered. Suffice to say, my brother, that pre-existence of the soul is a tale passed down from greatly imaginative minds and utterings of ancient times.*
>
> *Whereas the Father Fragment has gone through excellent training, and may have had many lifetimes of 'temporary accompanying experiences' prior to indwelling the person that is you, the soul is always an entirely new entity, a seed, a gift, for a cooperative human mind and perfect Father Fragment to develop into a new*

Eastern Beliefs.

being that will survive your passing away, and to which there is attached no original karma, good or bad.

I trust that in this talk we have put to rest the belief of pre-existing souls, and alleviated some of the associated disquiet in those individuals that are accepting of bad karma, perhaps accumulated in carelessly lived previous soul lives. [15]

It is interesting that Andrea says that even they do not always know where the past life memory comes from, although she has guided mankind for about half of the time we have existed on Earth. She also comments that our minds have the ability to reach out, and find historic events, and then take those as being our own, simply because of the way they appear to us – literally through our eyes. I guess that illustrates that we will never totally tie this subject down. (More information on Midwayers can be found in the Urantia Book.)

What evidence is there for the existence of this Indwelling Spirit? Well, this is very hard to prove, naturally, but there have been a number of individuals who have managed to establish a communication with their Indwelling Spirit. If you read these transmissions, they are clearly speaking from a divine perspective.

One such source, only very recently published[16], and which can be found on this web site www.1111angels.com, includes the following:

A Thought Adjuster Speaks – 2 January
Feel my total acceptance of you.

Yes, stand in awe before me -- I, who give everlasting life to each of my children. Allow self to be totally saturated in my love.

It is I, who abides in you and with you. All the days of this life count as nothing, compared to the Life I have prepared for you.

You are my child. Even before I created you, I had a special plan and purpose for your life. Your life is meant to

---

[15] Reincarnation – A Myth. https:// new-birth.net/link1/
[16] *The Guiding Light Within* by Lytske published by 11:11 Publishers ISBN 978-09577889-8-5

> sing praises unto me, and in your doing so, you sing praises to yourself.
> For know this my child: I AM you and you are becoming me. Together we are as one. You live your life, to become one with me.
> Feel my total acceptance of you. Let me flow through you. Let me guide you into life everlasting.
> Oh Joy! Oh Love! Oh Life!

Another possible contender for having been written by a Indwelling Spirit is a popular book amongst orthodox Christians. This is "God Calling."[17] I recently learnt that the books authored by Eva B. Werber[18] also appeal to be communications from her Indwelling Spirit, although she never made that connection. However that is certainly the conclusion of people who have read them, and are familiar with the concept. Some of these books are: "In His Presence", "Journey With the Master", "Quiet Talks With the Master", and "Voice of the Master". These date back to 1936.

Sylvia Browne, who passed on 20th Nov 2013 was a relatively well known psychic and has appeared on TV, has written a book, "Life on the Other Side." This little gem caught my eye. Francine, Sylvia Browne's guide can actually see the Indwelling Spirit, and has some limited ideas about this:

> The spirits at home are alerted that we're on our way when, as Francine describes it, our light begins blinking, the light of God we each carry inside us that acts almost literally as a "pilot light" to keep our soul illuminated, our own "eternal torch."[19]

Her term "Pilot Light" is indeed one of the names for the Indwelling Spirit. The Urantia Book also tells that spirits can see the divine light it

---

[17] *God Calling*, edited by A.J.Russell, published by The Berkley Publishing Group, ISBN 0-515-09026-3
[18] *In His Presence* by Eva Bell Werber published by De Vorss Publications (1946) ISBN 9780875161020
[19] *Life on The Other Side,* Published by Judy Piatkus (Publishers) Limited in 2000. ISBN 0-7499-2182-X page 74.

Eastern Beliefs.

gives off, but this was the first time I had seen such a thing reported outside that book. The kind of verification I love to find.

But since there are many sources of such "inner voices" how can you tell that any particular voice is a Indwelling Spirit? I think the honest answer is that there are not, and have never been many folk hearing Indwelling Spirits, and when you do stumble across one, you will be sure the source of their guidance is very special indeed. The irony is we all have such special guidance, but so very few of us can actually hear the words. That is not to suggest Indwelling Spirits are ineffective, simply that they remain unidentified.

If you have the experience of hearing an "inner voice", this is not typically an audible voice with an accent or tone. It is simply a string of thoughts. Thoughts don't have a tone. Most of us rightly assume what appears in your mind is your own creation – your own thoughts. I can recall one instance when a thought appeared in my mind that was so out of context that I immediately knew it came from somewhere else. But there have been other instances when I truly believed the thought I had was my own, only to be told it was spirit initiated. So, mostly we can't tell where our thoughts come from.

I can hear a very quiet "inner voice." How can I tell this is my Indwelling Spirit and not some passing spirit? In my case I can get answers to questions before I pose the question. I hear a "yes" or "no" as fast as a flash right as I start to compose the question. And I know that I cannot fool the "answer" by changing the structure of the question. I do not know of any spirits who are capable of that anticipation, as it requires a vision of the future, or perhaps, complete integration with my mind. Such are Indwelling Spirits.

So in this chapter I have proposed that the transfer of those life memories from one Indwelling Spirit, who guided the now deceased spiritual leader, to the Indwelling Spirit of the young child whose destiny is to take the lead role in that spiritual group, is the explanation of why some incredibly spiritually advanced individuals believe that they have been reincarnated. In a way they have – they have had deposited in their minds the previous life experiences of their "predecessor." But that situation only pertains to a very small number of people, but I suspect that this may have been a large factor in the development of this belief in the Eastern parts of the World.

Even the case of those who are gifted an experienced Indwelling Spirit, only pertains to certain people. It may not apply to you or me. However I am led to believe that ever more experienced Indwelling Spirits are appearing on our world. This is apparently related to the so called "Indigo" children – remarkably gifted children. So perhaps it is becoming more common. I will return to the topic of spirit sources later, when discussing thought transfer as a potential source of past life memories. I certainly am not suggesting that Indwelling Spirits are responsible for the majority of past life experiences. But they will have had an impact in some very influential situations. And as such, had a more than proportionate effect on large numbers of people.

In Chapter 4 we will talk about the more common sources of past life memories.

Chapter 2

The Bible.

Many in the West have come to see reincarnation as a "second chance" and thus far fairer than the orthodox Christian belief of only one chance, with many of us apparently consigned to an eternity of darkness or fire. Clearly, reincarnation cannot be true at the same time as an **eternal** hell. If the purpose of reincarnation is to sort out "karma" and pay back your debts, then there is no need for a "hell." Particularly since karma is supposed to be worked out here on Earth. Indeed, if you survived a "hell" and then had karmic debt to resolve on Earth, how fair would that be? Conversely, if we keep on coming back here, then we can't be stuck in an **eternal** hell. So the **eternal** hell concept has to go, if you accept reincarnation as a belief. No bad thing, to be honest. And more than likely you would also reject any version of hell, even if it is not eternal.

So, coming back here, to work out your failures, is certainly a lot more pleasant a prospect than an eternity in darkness. I do wonder if the rapid acceptance of reincarnation in the West is directly related to fundamentalist and evangelical Christians spreading their doctrine of eternal punishment. But, no matter how many people believe in something, that is of itself no proof of its veracity. On the other hand, it does mean it should not be rejected without due consideration. Of course if you rejected the eternal part of the hell concept to start with, then you would have no need to adopt reincarnation as a concept to get you out of a troublesome bit of Christian dogma. Well I guess it's only troublesome to those that see the Creator as all-loving. We will return to the topic of hell later, in Chapter 11.

People do sometimes point to the Bible, and find therein some apparent references to reincarnation. It is indeed true that in the early years of Christianity there was a group promoting this belief. But that should not really surprise you, because in the first 300 years of Christianity there were a great many diverse views about what it was that Jesus actually taught. That was sorted out in the year 325 at the Council of Nicaea, at the time of Emperor Constantine, and reinforced, often at the end of a sword, for the next thousand years. This of course does not mean that reincarnation is false; it simply means that many dissenting views were silenced at that time. And at that time there were a wide range of views about what Jesus taught, and indeed, who he really was. After the Council of Nicea, anything not codified was deemed heresy. Finally you could say what being an orthodox Christian meant from the point of view of belief.

But is there anything in the Bible today that supports reincarnation? People have pointed to a number of phrases, but I can't say I have been overly impressed by any of these. A favourite is Jesus saying *"Before Abraham, I am"*. I would not suggest that simply because one source, such as the Bible, makes such a statement, it means the concept is true. I am also not suggesting that all of a "sacred" text like the Bible is false. Indeed personally I do find much in the Bible that is true for me. To take this quotation specifically, I have no trouble explaining it. It would appear that "Jesus" was indeed someone unusual. You can read The Urantia Book to get a different insight into that, although of course orthodox Christians certainly believe he is unique. All that is necessary to put a very plain meaning to this phrase is to accept that Jesus was alive as a conscious entity prior to being born as a man. So, he probably did say, with absolute veracity: *"Before Abraham, I am."* I have no doubt all such interpretations in the Bible have explanations, even if that explanation is that the translation as recorded in today's English versions of the Bible is inaccurate, or totally false.

Some folks then suggest that if Jesus was "alive" before he came here, surely that suggests reincarnation? Not so. Reincarnation means coming back here to this Earth again and again until you have reached a sufficient level of spiritual maturity to move on. Even very advanced spiritual beings are sometimes said to "return" one more time just to teach us. While what I believe about Jesus may not be your cup of tea, unless it can be proved that he has lived at least two mortal lives here, that point cannot be substantiated. Many would be willing to consider at the very least, that he might have been an "Avatar", or an advanced spiritual teacher, and that would be a good description of my personal belief.

The Bible.

Of course there are phrases in the Bible like – *"And as it is appointed unto men once to die"*[20]– which seems a pretty straightforward denial of reincarnation. Then of course folks talk about Lazarus. He was supposed to have died, and been brought back to life by Jesus, so he must have died twice? Even if you believe that to be accurate, I doubt it really makes for much in the way of proof of reincarnation. After all Lazarus continued in the same mortal frame, he did not return as a baby.

What about the case of John the Baptist being said to have been a reincarnation of Elias? Well Elias came back in 1917 to deny that, but I suppose you might not believe that. On the other hand, I doubt you would be reading any of this if you were not somewhat open to spirit communication, so having a look at what Elias is supposed to have said to James Padgett might be worthwhile:

> *I was Elijah of the Old Testament, and I actually lived and was a prophet among the Jews, and was not John the Baptist, nor was he a reincarnation of me as some of Earth teachers claim. John was himself alone. He was in the flesh only once and was not a reincarnation of me or anyone else.*[21]

There is also the Biblical story of Elias appearing at the transfiguration on the mount, together with Moses, which was probably not long after John the Baptist's death – although there is great controversy around the actual year of his death. So on the face of it; it seems very unlikely that John the Baptist and Elias were the same being, else John the Baptist would surely have been the one in the transfiguration scene?

Sylvia Browne goes to some length to explain how she arrives at her belief in reincarnation, and interestingly, quotes her favourite item from the bible, to illustrate that it "originally" supported reincarnation. So, I better address that one too. She quotes John, Chapter 9:

> *"Master who did sin, this man or his parents, that he was born blind?"*

---

[20] Hebrews 9:27
[21] Elias was not John the Baptist – https:// new-birth.net/link2/ February 7th, 1917

Is Reincarnation an Illusion?

Sylvia takes that verse to suggest that since he was born blind, his being blind from birth must have been karma from a previous life, since he surely would have been sinless at birth. A clever argument, but I think flawed. Sylvia has not yet read James Padgett, who channeled some of the most amazing stuff ever received. It seems that sadly sins of our fathers (and mothers) do indeed influence the soul condition of babies. We are unfortunately not born without sin, or perhaps more accurately, the effects of sin, in this case our parent's sin.[22]

In some spiritual way, being born to parents who have sinned, affects our soul condition, and we do not come into this life without blemish. This explanation has however **nothing** to do with the Christian concept of original sin, I should state. Having given you that explanation, I would not go the next step and suggest that being born blind is a result of any specific transgression by the child's parents, but on the other hand, I understand that many of our physical ills and frailties are caused by the degenerate spiritual condition of mankind in general. If you read the Bible carefully you will discover around the time of Adam and Eve folks seemed to live a very much longer life span than we do now. Apparently as we slid into sin, this has had an effect on our physical bodies, how long we live, and the diseases that affect us. But a specific sin was not the cause of that birth defect.

In fact this was channeled by Dr. Samuels[23] in response to that very passage, and in response to it being a favourite passage of those who believe in reincarnation:

> The child born blind did not sin, nor did its parents, but suffered blindness because of the physical defect in his mother, which prevented the perfect development of the foetus in her womb, and thus this defect has prevented the perfect manifestation of God's work of creation. This defect is one of many to which the imperfect world of the flesh is subject, and it is for this reason that purification of the soul while in the flesh would be a task of countless centuries, and a punishment worse than the most evil hells of the spirit world in its duration.

---

[22] "The sins of the parents are visited upon the children unto the third and fourth generations." https://new-birth.net/link3/ received by James Padgett on April 9th, 1916
[23] Dr. Samuels was the next significant medium to follow James Padgett and continue the same concepts and contact with similar spirit entities.

Here the spirit comments on how difficult it would be to attain purification on this world and that it might take "countless centuries." I have often wished that I could create a mathematical model of the spiritual progress of the Earth and its beings, which I see as almost negligible over the last 2,000 years, and thus prove that if there is any reincarnation going on, the souls are not managing to advance significantly. Indeed applying the law of averages, some must be going backwards. Even looking around for substantial numbers of very advanced spiritual beings, which one would expect to be on their last incarnation, these folks are very hard to find. Sure we can always find some stunning examples, but not substantial numbers. And for those we can always find the opposite, huge numbers of materially orientated or evil minded folks.

While applying "logic" to this topic of reincarnation, one should mention that where the theory fails most spectacularly, is in the issue of the loss of memory which surely should not accompany any important learning experience. We arrive here with clean memory banks[24], which is indeed why we tend to believe that anything we find in our local mind must be our own experience. Proponents then suggest that it is after death that we review the past experience, and choose new experiences. Well, what we will see is that typically after death folks can review their immediately previous life, but it's rare to recall any other incarnation, although given enough determination, something will emerge. But that does not in my view prove anything. As we will see later, almost anything can be traversed to deliver up a memory. And the more you are determined to achieve that, the more certain it is you will.

---

[24] The issue of young children and their "past life memories" is discussed at length in Chapter 5.

Chapter 3

Where is the mind?

While this may seem an odd topic to introduce, I think that one of the issues many people have with trying to figure things out is that they still adhere to the notion that the mind is in the brain, and all those thoughts simply rattle around there. Of course that is what many psychiatrists and other scientists still teach.

But some recent researchers have uncovered some facts that will certainly startle you, if you have not been keeping abreast of things. Dean Radin recently wrote "Entangled Minds"[25] and as one reviewer says:

> *"The implications of Radin's premises are majestic. His views strike at the heart of the notion of the isolated individual, and replace it with an image of the unity of all minds. Radin shows that togetherness does not have to be developed; it already exists and needs only to be realized."*

One of the really neat things he does in that book is add together the probabilities of all the experiments on particular topics to arrive at an overall statistic that reflects the probability that psi effects are real. This is 1.3×10^{104} to 1. That is overwhelming. However if you follow each experiment closely, you will see that in pretty much all cases, while the odds favour the existence of a psi effect, it's so small that it's pretty much useless. Thus the folks that he uses to discern whether they can alter the throw of a dice would probably be hardly ahead if they were betting on it. But he mentions other stunning facts. That the events of both the twin towers on Sept 11 2001, and the death of Princess Diana on 31st August 1997 caused random number generators to malfunction. In other words, the huge emotion manifested upset these machines. Machines which are designed to create random numbers, and which are tested mathematically to ensure that is what they are doing.

---

[25] *"Entangled Minds"* by Dean Radin published by Paraview Pocket Books, ISBN 978-1-4165-1677-4

Is Reincarnation an Illusion?

Now I will move to Rupert Sheldrake, and his experiments with cats and dogs, as an intriguing proof of the weirdness of the human mind. On the internet (YouTube) there is an hour and a half long video, which is well worth watching.

Rupert Sheldrake[26] has researched the often reported phenomenon of pets being found waiting by the front door. In the past we ascribed this to acute hearing and recognizing the sounds of owners or their cars, but by using video cameras, he is able to prove that the pets start waiting for their owner the moment the owner decides to return home, even if that is an hour away, and the owner is a considerable distance away. It is clear that cats and dogs are attuned to the thoughts of their owners. Clearly those thoughts are emerging from their minds, and travelling to the pets. Or the pets are going out and looking for the thoughts. Either way, they are connecting in a way we did not previously know about.

There is a third option, which is in line with Quantum Mechanics and its concept of entanglement, and that is that they are at all times connected. If cats and dogs can read our thoughts, surely we mortals can too? In fact I had the opportunity to observe my ex-wife doing precisely that in respect of our only son, and subsequently verified that she was correct in respect of the issue, and the timing. In my own case, after my mother passed over, I spent a lot of time talking to her; perhaps "lecturing" would be more apt a description. When a gifted friend channeled her words, she soon asked me to stop talking to her. Quite obviously she had received my thoughts across the veil, and I was becoming tiresome! I realize both of these personal stories are anecdotes, and cannot be considered proof, but as I mentioned earlier, I will discuss many things that cannot be considered proof. That per se does not mean they are wrong, simply that some folks will prefer not to believe that they may be true. But others may be more open-minded.

I recently read a wonderful book – if you love African animals. This is the Elephant Whisperer[27]. The creator of a private wild life reserve in South Africa adopts a totally wild and out of control herd of elephants that would otherwise have been shot. He spends a great deal of time, even at some personal risk, to connect with them, and get them to stay on his reserve,

---

[26] *The Extended Mind: Recent Experimental Evidence* by Rupert Sheldrake, a presentation http://www.youtube.com/watch?v=JnA8GUtXpXY

[27] *the elephant whisperer* by Lawrence Anthony published by Pan Books ISBN 978-0-330-50668-7

rather than try to return to their original homeland. There are a number of amazing stories in that book, but the one that is pertinent is in respect of this herd's ability to sense when he was not on the reserve, and to meet him on his return. The elephants would be somewhere on the reserve, yet they would be able to time their arrival at the living quarters, to his return. But a truly amazing event occurred. The elephants appeared, sensing his return, but he missed his flight from Johannesburg, and at the precise time that happened, the elephants went back into the bush, to reappear again timed to his actual but delayed arrival. So not only did they know when he planned to arrive, but when he missed his flight, and was about 600 km away, they knew. This cannot be explained by minds trapped in a physical brain.

There is a sequel to this book that is just as amazing. The author passed away on March 7th 2012. Yet on March 10th three days after his death they all arrived to pay their respects in the same way as they mourn the loss of their own, and stayed without eating, before going back to the bush.

This short chapter is meant simply as an introduction to the notion that minds are not purely of the material of the brain. I could divert into a more detailed discussion on the subject of mind, but it's beyond the scope of this book. From my perspective we have a local mind that is located about the head, and is very closely interlinked with the brain, much as a TV set receives many channels from TV stations. Precisely what the structure and location of Universal Mind is, I am far less sure. There may be many such repositories, but we will certainly discuss some aspects of Universal Mind, also called the Akashic Record in later chapters.

Chapter 4

Past Life Memories.

Moving on, what of the very large numbers of folk who report "past life" memories. This must be the area that has the most impact on people, as some of these memories have been well researched and they present as very intriguing tales. Studies have even been done of children, and they too have "past life memories". In fact I have no doubt at all, that were I to submit to hypnosis, I too would come up with "past life" memories. The vast majority of hypnotherapists are, I suspect, firm believers in reincarnation. So I rather fancy taking the work of some of these, and using their own examples against them.

I will start with Sylvia Browne, and her book "Life on the Other Side."[28] It's an interesting book, no doubt about that. Apparently Sylvia gets most of her information from her guide Francine. Sylvia is herself a hypnotherapist, so she also has that side to her experiences. That Francine believes in reincarnation would not greatly surprise me, although I gather she does not claim (in that book at least) to have had any further lives since her life ended in 1520. It is not entirely clear from that particular book whether she does or does not support reincarnation.

As far as I can tell, a very large number of spirits particularly in the lower Spirit Spheres do believe in reincarnation. This should not surprise anyone who studies spirit, because we do not change just because we arrive in spirit. And given the large number of humans who believe in reincarnation, it follows that spirits will too. While I have heard many humans claim to have actually had past lives, this particular point is not so common in spirit. It occurs, but in my experience spirits normally say it hasn't happened to them - yet. But they expect it will soon.

In passing there is a source of channeled messages with some very ancient – maybe over 5000 years old – spirits who claim not to have

---

[28] *"Life on The Other Side"* by Sylvia Browne.

Is Reincarnation an Illusion?

reincarnated yet. And of course that is the problem. How do you know that you are never going to reincarnate? How long should you wait before deciding it won't happen? In at least one case, 3000 years was not long enough, but the spirit in question was puzzled. Of course some may say: "Well he perhaps had progressed enough so that he didn't have to!" But the point is that he said he had only had one Earth life, and that would destroy the view that we need to have dozens if not hundreds of lives to have all the possible permutations of experience.

> *And this I must say, that in all the centuries of my spirit existence, never have I known a spirit or the soul of a spirit to reincarnate, and in this my disappointment has been grievous. Many spirits of our association have become perfect through renunciation, and yet they have remained spirits and progressed to the highest heavens of our possibilities (the Sixth Sphere).*
>
> *Yet, strange as it may seem in view of this experience, we still, to a more or less degree, cling to our old beliefs in reincarnation, thinking that there is something else, that we know not of, to be done in order for reincarnation to become the destiny of our souls.*
>
> *Sometimes I think that my beliefs in this particular must be wrong, for in comparing the condition of mortals, the most advanced in their mind and soul development, I realize that they are not in a small degree the equal of us in development, and then I wonder and, wondering, cannot understand what good could be accomplished or what improvement made in our condition for progressing, should we again enter mortal bodies.*
>
> *As true theosophy taught, as we conceived it, reincarnation was a supposed process of purification, and necessary in order that the spirit could attain to a state of perfection and freedom from everything that defiles his soul and prevents that soul from arriving at the blissful state of Nirvana, which means only that condition of soul where no longer reincarnation is necessary or possible; and when I know that many of our spirits - one time believers in these doctrines - have arrived at that condition and entered a state of perfect happiness, I hesitate longer to believe, and only hold the faith because*

> *I fear that the experience mentioned may be the results of special circumstances.*
>
> *But if I cease to believe these teachings, what shall I believe? No one can tell me that this reincarnation will not take place, and I fear to surrender the belief.*
>
> *I further believe that in order for the workings of karma, as the doctrines hold, reincarnation is necessary - that only in the mortal body could I do the reaping that my sowing demands, and yet, I see and know that karma has been and is working in this spirit world, to the extent that the reaping has all been accomplished, and the spirit made perfect, and this without any reincarnation; for as I have said, never have I known or heard of the reincarnation of a spirit or of anything that is connected with or represents the spirit.*[29]

This ancient spirit, by name Lamlestia, no longer sees any need for karma after all his years in the spirit realm. In other words, he has progressed way beyond the point at which he came into the spirit world. He no longer carries any "baggage"; he is in effect, purified, or perfect, and has achieved this while in spirit. Even this would destroy the basis of reincarnation, because the theory is that you resolve karma here, and must leave this Earth perfect, in order to end the cycle of reincarnation. But here this spirit is saying he was able to resolve his imperfections while in spirit. And if that is true, then the karma side of things being resolved on Earth, is not true.

But to get back to past life memories. If you read Sylvia's book: "Life on the Other Side", she tells of the existence of Akashic records. She also explains that not only can you visit a great hall of records in the next realm, but you can "put these on" in some fashion that enables one to totally experience that individual's life. Here is a quote from that book:

> *"It was from Rahein that I first learned about the extraordinary option of merging with a chart in the Hall*

---

[29] Lamlestia (an ancient spirit) discusses reincarnation and theosophy. https://new-birth.net/link4/ received by James Padgett on December 17th, 1916.

Is Reincarnation an Illusion?

> of Records as an incredibly effective research tool. Raheim is a passionate historian, and one day he was studying the life of General George Custer and decided to merge with Custer's chart. Suddenly, as he described it, he found himself in the midst of charging horses and chaotic war cries, his whole being thrilled with the terror and adrenaline of battle, his throat burning from the acrid clouds of gunpowder. Intellectually, he knew he wasn't actually living the battle or in any real danger from it. But that didn't diminish its impact on his senses and his awareness that for those several moments he'd been given very intimate, "firsthand" knowledge of everything Custer thought, felt, heard and saw in the final moments of his life.[30]

So, Sylvia "proves" the existence of "Universal Memory," and one's ability to tap into this, and also the incredible multi-dimensional nature of it – it literally covers all the senses. A point to note here that this memory recall is totally unlike the normal memory recalls we have of real memories in our own "local" mind. No matter how unique the experience, I have never heard anyone describe a real personal memory with this multi-dimensional nature. Think about lunch yesterday. That memory recall is certainly not a multidimensional sensory experience. But I have read accounts of "past life" memories that are described in just such a multi-sensory fashion. Which fact folks often point to as proof of its veracity. Well it may be a very convincing recall, but it is much more likely to prove it's **not** a local memory. Yet it seems that most who have these experiences, and see, hear, sense and feel events through their own senses are in fact convinced it is their personal memory. I wonder why Rahein knew it was not his past life? Perhaps because of the way it was introduced, as an Akashic Record?

This is no surprise to me. I have a feeling that all thoughts are essentially eternal in nature, and stored somewhere. But thoughts are not simply "brain waves". These thoughts can have attached full sound, video, smell, and even taste to them – all the emotions in fact. You really do have a three dimensional, multi-sensual record available, probably for all time. This, I suspect is what many people tap into simply by being hypnotized. What happens under hypnotism is that

---

[30] *Life on the Other Side,* by Sylvia Browne, page 106.

one falls into a deep trance precisely like that achieved in deep meditation by those who channel. Of course some folks can channel in a waking state, like John Edward, but far more people need to achieve some degree of trance, even a light trance, in order to connect with spirit.

But it seems it is not just human thoughts that are available in this fashion. I will skip now to another amazing book "Letters from a living dead man"[31]. This is a book taken from the experiences of a spirit during his first year on the other side. The spirit in question, Judge David Patterson Hatch, was born in Dresden Maine, on November 22nd, 1846. He died in Los Angeles on February 21st, 1912. He was a firm believer in reincarnation as a human, and naturally, in spirit he still had that belief.

This book was channeled in 1912 and 1913 by Elsa Barker, a friend of David Hatch, who lived in Europe. She discovered that she was able to record messages from a spirit, by a method called automatic writing, where the pen appeared to have a life of its own. In fact not only did she not initially know the source of the message, she also did not know that David Hatch was dead. She was based in Paris at the time, and had not heard of his passing till later. She was not a spiritualist either by inclination or experience. This was a totally novel experience for her, save only that she had frequently seen visions that proved to be prophetic.

From this series of "letters" the book was constructed. It is important to note that Judge David Hatch, the spirit author, was a learned man, and one of some spiritual development. He wrote a number of books on Hinduism, under an assumed name. In "real" life he was a renowned advocate and judge. Suffice it to say he believed in reincarnation while here, and had not changed his view after passing over.

David Hatch has this to say about a young fellow Lionel, who is about twelve years of age, that he meets up with in spirit:

> *I advise him not to be in any hurry about going back. The curious thing about it is that he can remember other*

---

[31] A free pdf is available here: https://new-birth.net/link5/ and will be used as the page number references.

Is Reincarnation an Illusion?

> *and former lives of his on Earth. Many out here have no more memory of their former lives, before the last one, than they had while in the body. This is not a place where everyone knows everything–far from it. Most souls are nearly as blind as they were in life.*[32]

This of course disagrees with what Lamlestia had to say, that he had not ever met anyone in spirit who had any memory of a previous life. But young Lionel has more to intrigue us about. He too seems to believe he has had a previous life, but David Hatch does at one point say:

> *"Most of the men and women here do not know that they have lived many times in flesh. They remember their latest life more or less vividly, but all before that seems like a dream."*[33]

He later explains that these past life memories must be recovered, because they are not "top of mind." He says further:

> *If a man understands that his recent sojourn on Earth was merely the latest of a long series of lives, and if he concentrates his mind towards recovering the memories of the distant past, he can recover them. Some persons may think that the mere dropping of the veil of matter should free the soul from all obscuration; but, as on Earth so out here, "things are not thus and so because they ought to be, but because they are."*[34]

I will first relate the story of a deep meditation because this extends the idea of Universal Memory a stage further. David Hatch says:

> *Here, if I choose, I can spend hours in watching the changing colours of a cloud. Or, better still, I can lie on my back and remember. It is wonderful to remember, to let the mind go back year after year, life after life, century after century, back and back till one finds oneself – a turtle! But one can look ahead, forward and forward, life*

---

[32] *Letters from a living dead man*, Letter 11, page 29.
[33] *Letters from a living dead man*, Letter 16, page 46.
[34] *Letters from a living dead man*, Letter 17, page 53.

> *after life, century after century, eon after eon, till one finds oneself an archangel.*[35]

Considering that one evolved from a turtle is pretty way out, but the conclusion that we might evolve into an archangel is even more intriguing. Of course the good David Hatch could not read The Urantia Book, because it was only published in 1955. So he would not know that archangels are created that way. They do not evolve from anything less, whether angelic or mortal. We mortals apparently have an unlimited growth path ahead, but we will not turn into archangels, or any other angelic form.

Perhaps one could simply forgive his use of the word, and consider it just a matter of poor word selection? But evolving from turtles? Well The Urantia Book covers that too, but I thought it was a frog actually. It really does not matter a great deal, unless I suppose one is concerned about how accurate these mind trips through time might be. And I guess some folks would be very concerned about that. Later David Hatch talks about meditation:

> *The other night I was meditating on a flower seed, for there is nothing so small that it may not contain a world. I was meditating on a flower seed, and amusing myself by tracing its history, generation by generation, back to the dawn of time. I smile as I use that figure, "the dawn of time," for time has had so many dawns and so many sunsets, and still it is unwearied.*[36]

This immediately made me think: if you can indeed meditate on a seed back though the mists of time, then you can do that very thing with your own body. Of course our body is being refreshed at the molecular level literally every few months. I gather we don't have any "old" molecules in terms of our human body, except in as much as molecules are never destroyed, so they are all as old as creation. So where do these trips through time come from? It doesn't seem likely it is molecular memory. Certainly some have suggested as much. So it's an appropriate point to digress on another "past life" memory that has been well researched.

---

[35] *Letters from a living dead man,* Letter 26, page 87.
[36] *Letters from a living dead man,* Letter 41, page 168.

Is Reincarnation an Illusion?

Here I refer to research by Stanislav Grof, M.D. He was a researcher into altered states of consciousness, and initially this involved conducting therapy with psychedelic substances, first in Czechoslovakia, in the Psychiatric Research Institute in Prague, and then in the United States, at the Maryland Psychiatric Research Center in Baltimore, MD, where he participated in the last surviving official American psychedelic research program. Not only did he have patients whose memories could not have come via DNA or cellular memory, but some had memories of "animals" clearly not a source of DNA or cellular tissue at all for a human.

One of his interesting cases was a lady by the name of Renata:

> She experienced a number of episodes that took place in seventeenth century Prague, at a crucial period in Czech history. After the disastrous battle of White Mountain in 1621, which marked the beginning of the Thirty Years' War in Europe, the country ceased to exist as an independent kingdom and came under the hegemony of the Hapsburg dynasty. In an effort to destroy the feelings of national pride and to defeat the forces of resistance, the Hapsburgs sent out mercenaries to capture the country's most powerful noblemen. Twenty-seven prominent aristocrats were arrested and beheaded in a public execution on a scaffold erected in the Old Town Square in Prague.
>
> During her historical sessions, Renata had an unusual variety of images and insights concerning the architecture of the experienced period and typical garments and costumes, as well as weapons and various utensils used in everyday life. She was also able to describe many of the complicated relationships existing at that time between the royal family and the vassals. Renata had never specifically studied this period of Czech history or was interested in it. I had to go to the library and do historical research in order to confirm that the information Renata reported was accurate.[37]

---

[37] From http://www.scribd.com/doc/19348349/Evidence-for-the-Akashic-Field-From-Modern-Consciousness-Research

Subsequently Renata was able to discover that this individual was in fact in her family tree, but had died without fathering any children, thus wiping out any possibility that her memory was DNA or cellular based. So the source of this memory was something else. In the case of this researcher, he believes it to be the Akashic Field – what I would call Universal Mind or Akashic Records.

Indeed as we discussed earlier, if all past lives are recorded in Universal Memory, and all you need is some trigger to lead you on a merry journey, you can in fact play all manner of mind games, traversing time. This very point was made by Judas, when questioned on the issue of "thought objects." Yes this is the same Judas of the Bible, who else would admit to that name?

> [Medium.: In the context of "thought containers" I had seen, already some days ago, the image of a pink rose, like one of those I have in my garden. And the voice told me: "This is not just the image of some rose; it is not a generic flower, but it is a very specific rose. It is a thought that - besides the image -contains more information: The fragrance of the flower, if the thinker has really smelled its aroma; the silky touch of its petals, if the thinker has really touched them; the hardness of its thorns, if the thinker has really tried them; the green color of its leaves, if the thinker has really paid attention to them. And this thought is connected with other thoughts: it refers to the garden where it grows, to its owner, to the land where it lives. This thought is like a knot in a tissue of thoughts, and starting from this point, you may easily arrive at other points or thoughts, and so you may succeed in penetrating ever deeper into the thinker's mental world.
> "God also has thoughts. And if you are able to capture one of them, and if you succeed in following their thread and their context, you will come ever closer to Him".]
> [Judas] My dear brother,
> There is not one thought that disappears, and all are accessible to us, and you can access all that are on your level or below. Apart from what you received in the vision of the rose, thoughts also vibrate with emotional contents: they distill love, hatred, joy, fear - in short, all those

> emotions that the thinker felt in the moment of creating it. Therefore, many thoughts are attractive, because of their positive emotional contents; others are repulsive.
>
> It is the favorite hobby in the high spheres of the natural heavens to hunt these thoughts and to follow their threads, to travel along this fabric of individual life and to reconstruct or to revive the world of other people. More than a hobby, it is the centerpiece of their lives, their reason of being. They are able to contemplate any event of history from any angle of view. There are spirits who are dedicated - already for thousands of years - to this hunt, and they feel very happy. They have accumulated immense knowledge, on history, on languages and philosophies, and they have contributed their own thoughts in that respect.[38]

This message continues the overall concept of an accessible Akashic Record, the Universal Memory, that holds all thoughts, and that can be traversed in multiple directions, simply by the power of the mind. It seems there is no aspect that is not indexed, to use a computer database term. The ultimate searchable database, although Judas introduces a limitation – that we can only search thoughts produced by people at or below our current level of spiritual advancement. Those that are well versed in Internet searches may be familiar with the curious way by which you can go from subject to subject, and indeed how hard it can be to even stay focused on one topic. I tend to believe it is our ability to access this Akashic Record that provides the prime source of past life memories. But there are also other sources of memories.

We will return to this concept later, when I have introduced the idea of attached and other adjacent spirits. You might of course be thinking that maybe spirits can traverse the Akashic Record, but why should that apply to us? I think that some of the examples I will introduce concerning what we can do, should illustrate that we are spirit now.

---

[38] Thoughts continued. https://new-birth.net/link6/ received by the medium HR on June 30th, 2003

Past Life Memories.

The only significant difference between us and spirit is that we also have a mortal body.

In this chapter we have introduced the concept of an accessible universal store of past memories – something that can contain emotions, sounds and all the features to enable one to relive the event. And we have introduced the notion that it is all interconnected, and thus can be traversed effortlessly, all you need is some starting point, and off you will go. Readers of popular books like Brian Weiss[39] has written will be familiar with the curious way that his patients arrive at memories that do indeed seem to have a logical connection to the patient. We will return to this book "Same Soul, Many Bodies" later.

---

[39] *Same Soul, Many Bodies: Discover the Healing Power of Future Lives through Progression Therapy.* By Brian L. Weiss. Publisher Free Press (August 30, 2005) ISBN-13: 978-0743264341

Chapter 5

"Past Life" researcher Ian Stevenson.

The most well known of the researchers into the so called past life memories, would be Dr. Ian Stevenson (1918-2007). His best known book is "Twenty Cases Suggestive of Reincarnation" published in 1974. This book seems to have had a very large impact on the public at large, based simply on the number of people who have quoted it to me as proof of reincarnation. Ironically however, although Ian Stevenson dedicated his life to achieving that – i.e. proof, he was never as confident in his publications or his public statements. He never ever suggested that his research was "proof". Here is what he had to say on the matter, in a lecture given in 1989, for The Flora Levy Lecture in the Humanities:

> *Journalists have sometimes incorrectly (and unjustly) described me as trying to prove that reincarnation occurs. This allegation is wrong as a description both of my motive and of science. Outside of mathematics there is no proof in science; scientists make judgments about probabilities, and they rarely express themselves in statements of certainty. It is true that I search for stronger evidence than we now have for paranormal processes in the cases I study, and if that evidence points toward reincarnation I am not displeased. I have never hidden my interest in the results of my research. William James pointed out that "if you want an absolute duffer in an investigation, you must, after all, take the man who has no interest in its results...the most useful investigator...is always he whose eager interest in one side of a question is balanced by an equally keen nervousness lest he become deceived." The search for stronger evidence is therefore not with an aim at developing some coercive proof. Instead it recognizes that different persons*

Is Reincarnation an Illusion?

> *require different amounts and qualities of evidence before they alter their opinions.*[40]

It is pretty certain that Ian Stevenson's real aim was to obtain proof of our continued existence after death, rather than prove reincarnation true. He believed that the most promising evidence for life after death "has been that provided by children who claim to remember previous lives." To this end he studied in detail over 2,500 cases across the world, frequently in languages that he could not speak. This required him to use translators, and he has been criticized on this basis, because it meant that he was dependent upon someone whose work and even whose skills he could not test. Interviewer bias in this sort of situation, especially when working with children in the age of 2 to 3 years must be considered as a strong possibility, when the interviewer has not been trained to avoid this. Furthermore, the translator used in a number of the cases in his book was found to have been dishonest, and the first publisher did not proceed with publication, because of this very issue, delaying the publication. These cases were collected in 1961 in India and Sri Lanka, but Ian Stevenson returned to these cases later, to ensure the records were accurate, and achieved publication in 1966.

Ian Stevenson himself was most interested in those cases where a birthmark appeared to be linked to some incident in the "past life" memory. He felt these were really the most solid type of proof, and he had a number of these within his sample, including a small subset where there appeared to be two such marks. I will address this issue later. I think that a reasonable person, reading this book, will indeed be most impressed with the correlations that are discovered between the memories and the actual past life. For my part I do take this book as proof that at least some of these past life memories are based on real historic events.

However I am the more interested in those cases that he could not explain. Even if he had 2,500 cases that were strongly indicative of "past lives" it is the cases that he cannot explain that tell us the most. And in fact one of these I believe throws great doubt on his hypothesis.

---

[40] From http://www.medicine.virginia.edu/clinical/departments/psychiatry/sections/cspp/dops/publicationslinks/some-of-my-journeys-in-medicine.pdf

"Past Life" researcher Ian Stevenson.

Another interesting fact about his work is the large number of "past life" memories that involved a violent death:

> a high incidence of violent death in the persons whose lives the children remember. This feature occurs in the cases of all ten cultures for which we have examined groups of cases; although the incidence of violent death in the cases varies from one culture to another, it is far higher among the cases than in the general populations from which they are drawn.[41]

Now this issue has been noted as curious by Ian Stevenson himself, and other commentators, but as far as I know, none have drawn any useful further inference from this, although some suggestions have been made. However from my own studies I know that this sort of sudden death is exactly what leads to the deceased passing to the Astral Plane, rather than the Spirit Spheres, where it is extremely easy, and indeed common for attachment and obsession of a living mortal to occur. More details of the differences between these two spirit-world dimensions are contained in Chapter 16. And as we will study later, spirit obsession is one case where memories can be recalled from the attached entity and reported by the mortal. There is some evidence of this within his sample set. Spirit obsession is a less severe case than spirit possession. In the latter case, the original soul appears to have either little to no control, or only infrequent control of the actions of the physical body. In the case of obsession, the original soul is in control, but is influenced to a greater or lesser degree by the intruder. It is also possible to have a spirit attachment, with some or almost no noticeable influence. These issues are discussed further in Chapter 7 and 8.

Another common factor is that of dreams announcing the intention to reincarnate:

> Other recurrent features also vary from culture to culture. These include the occurrence of dreams in which a deceased person seems to announce to the dreamer the

---

[41] http://www.healthsystem.virginia.edu/internet/personalitystudies/publicationslinks/some-of-my-journeys-in-medicine.pdf - Stevenson 1989

Is Reincarnation an Illusion?

> *intention of being reborn (usually in the family of the dreamer), ...[42]*

This is another curious issue, and one which I address later in Chapter 7. Although I have not found many cases, a small number of spirits have been found who were determined to reincarnate, and appeared to be trying to actually make that happen – as opposed to letting it occur, if indeed it does occur. Dr Carl Wickland[43] has such cases in his book, as does Dr Ian Stevenson. Even Dr Irene Hickman[44] reported such a case. Again this lends credence to my assertion that some of these memories, particularly in the case of young children, may have been brought about by the presence of attached entities. But I have other explanations to offer which do not involve attached entities.

But to move to those cases from Ian Stevenson's book which he could not explain, and using a commentary written by Ernest Valea:

> *First, there is the case of an Indian boy named Jasbir[45], aged three and a half, who was very ill and lapsed into a coma which his family temporarily mistook for death. He revived a few hours later, and after several weeks displayed a completely transformed behavior, claiming to be a Brahmin named Sobha Ram, who died in an accident while he (Jasbir) was sick. Since Sobha Ram died when Jasbir was already three and a half years old, his "past-life recall" obviously cannot be a proof of reincarnation. More than that, the "reincarnation" of Ram's soul must have taken place even before he had physically died, according to the timing of his accident and the illness of Jasbir. For the previous 3.5 years both persons lived physically in nearby villages. While speaking through Jasbir, the "reincarnated Mr. Ram" said that he was advised by a saint to take cover in Jasbir's body. As a result, at a certain moment there were present two personalities in Jasbir's body: the one of the child and the one of Mr. Ram.*

---

[42] From http://www.medicine.virginia.edu/clinical/departments/psychiatry/sections/cspp/dops/publicationslinks/some-of-my-journeys-in-medicine.pdf
[43] *"30 Years among the dead."*
[44] *"Remote Depossession."*
[45] Case number 2 from *Twenty Cases Suggestive of Reincarnation*.

"Past Life" researcher Ian Stevenson.

> This suggests that it cannot be a case of reincarnation, but rather a possession of Jasbir's body by the so-called spirit of Mr. Ram.
>
> Second, there is the case of Lurancy Vennum[46], a one-year-old girl who began to display the personality of Mary Roff when she (Mary Roff) died. This situation lasted several months, while Mary Roff claimed to have occupied the vacated body of the little girl. After this period Mary Roff departed and Lurancy Vennum resumed control. The overlapping of personalities and messages displayed during that period are strong indications of possession, excluding any possibility of reincarnation. Ian Stevenson admits in his book that "other cases of the present group of 20 cases may be instances of similar 'possessing influences' in which the previous personality just happened to die well before the birth of the present personality's body" (p. 381).
>
> Third, there is the case of a Buddhist monk, Chaokhun Rajsuthajarn[47], who was born a day before the death of Nai Leng, the personality he claimed to have been in his previous life. Stevenson commented in an interview[48]: "I studied this case with much care but couldn't find an explanation for the discrepancy."[49]

The case of Ravi Shankar[50] in Ian Stevenson's book has an overlap of six months. In other words, Ashok Kumar was murdered six months before Ravi Shankar was born. In my understanding the incarnation of a soul typically occurs at about four months but does vary, so I personally would not call that a definite case of possession on the basis of the timing alone. But it would be a very unusual case of reincarnation, I would suspect, to be so hard on the heels of the past life, and it looks closer to possession. But the case of Jasbir is definitely not reincarnation.

---

[46] This is not a case researched by Ian Stevenson in this book, but obviously he was very familiar with the case, and refers to it in his conclusions.
[47] This is also not a case researched by Ian Stevenson in this book.
[48] Omni Magazine 10(4):76 (1988)
[49] http://www.comparativereligion.com/reincarnation1.html#02
[50] Case number 5 in *Twenty Cases Suggestive of Reincarnation*.

Is Reincarnation an Illusion?

What we have here are three cases that are unlikely to be reincarnation. Yet they appear to be very similar to those cases where the memory recall belongs to an individual that did die before the birth of the person with the recall – what could be described as reincarnation. But, in all three of these cases above, this is far more than a memory, because the living human now has an altered personality, and acts exactly as if it is the deceased person, before returning to the original personality. Also during the period of the change, the individual claimed to be the deceased person, never trying to claim that they were the living personality, although in the case of Jasbir, who was in the body of a very young child, he came to accept that he must live as Jasbir, not as Sobha Ram.

My explanation for how a possessing spirit controls a human, is that it exerts, by virtue of its will, and the submission of the host to control the physical faculties similarly to the way that the host does. However it cannot be exactly the same way, because in my understanding the host's soul is connected to the physical body by means of a silver chord, which is only broken on death. If, as I assert, the mind is not in the brain, there is lots of scope for the brain to receive mindal input from beings that are not the host soul. So, even if a spirit is not actually possessing or obsessing a mortal, it seems very likely to me that their mere presence close by can lead to an accessing of their own past life memories by the human. We have some examples of that later.

It seems to me that researchers into this phenomenon are trying to find a single explanation that will explain all these cases, whereas its very probable that a number of different situations are occurring, which are only superficially similar. However I think it's only fair to give due credit to Ian Stevenson as an extremely thorough and objective scientific researcher, who was happy to include things in his publication that he could not explain. He was not unaware of the concepts of possession, but seemed to have an expectation of how a possessing spirit should behave, which I find at variance from my own perspective. Indeed it is clear that Dr Stevenson dismissed some of the hypotheses that he considered on the basis that they did not cover all his documented cases. He certainly appeared to be looking for a single bullet to resolve them all.

"Past Life" researcher Ian Stevenson.

Now to the issue of birthmarks. In "30 Years among the Dead"[51] Dr Carl Wickland found a number of situations where living mortals who came to him exhibited physical ailments. When the obsessing spirit was removed, using a static electric shock, and subsequently cross questioned, these attached spirits were shown to be the real cause of the ailment. Here are a number of cases taken from Chapter IX of that book:

> *Spirits who are ignorant of having lost their physical bodies often hold firmly in mind the thought of their former physical condition and continue to suffer pain. This "error of the mortal mind" persists until an understanding of transition and spiritual laws is reached, when freedom from ideas of physical limitations is attained.*
>
> *When spirits who are under this delusion of suffering and disease come into the auras of mortals their condition is conveyed to the sensitives, and chronic lassitude, pseudo-illness and psychic invalidism result.*
>
> *These sensitives endure all the pain of the spirits' former physical condition, and ordinary methods of treatment fail to cure, for the only permanent relief is found through the dislodgement of the ignorant entities.*
>
> *While we were in Chicago a friend of ours, Miss F. W., a companion to Mrs. McA, a prominent modiste in the city, asked us to concentrate for Mrs. McA., who was a chronic invalid. The latter had been ordered by her physicians to take a rest cure and could not be induced to get up again. She was suffering intense pains in the head and was subject to many changeable moods. Miss F. W. and Mrs. McA.'s masseuse were present during the following occurrence.*

EXPERIENCE, APRIL 2, 1908
Spirit: **GRACE BRUSTED Patient: MRS. McA**
Psychic: **MRS. WICKLAND**
(By way of explanation it is Mrs. Wickland who allows the displaced entity to talk through her.)

---

[51] *"30 Years among the Dead"* by Dr Carl Wickland, M.D. Newcastle Publishing Company Inc. (1974) ISBN 0-87877-025-9 but first published in 1924.

> The spirit at first spoke with great difficulty and complained of being very sick and was unable to sit up. She insisted that she was too sick to be up and wished to go to bed.
>
> When asked whether she knew anyone in the room she at once recognized Mrs. McA's masseuse and demanded that she take her to bed immediately, wait upon her and draw down the shades, as the light was too strong for a sick person.
>
> She gave her name as Grace Brusted, of Boston, said she was a Universalist, and that the year was 1898.
>
> She had been sick for a long time and felt as if she were two persons, at times herself and at other times another person.
>
> She was often called Mrs. McA., but was tired of answering to that name, as she did not like Mrs. McA. Recently she had had to do entirely too much work, having had to give orders to the sewing girls; furthermore, Miss F. W. would have to do things in her way or be discharged.
>
> The spirit repeated again that she was tired of living a double life, that she could not understand it and was more than ready to die.
>
> The way of progression was then explained and the spirit's grandmother and mother appeared to her, saying that she had always been a spoiled child, but would now have to learn to serve others.
>
> Miss F. W. and the masseuse said that Mrs. McA. had been acting in the same manner as this spirit, even using the identical language, and they later reported that on the following morning Mrs. McA. was in a very genial mood, remarking that it was, the first time for many months that she had wakened without a headache.
>
> After this she improved rapidly, left her bed and resumed her usual activities.

> For over a period of six years, a friend of ours, an elderly gentleman, eighty-four years old, was afflicted with unaccountable pains in the back of the neck and a

"Past Life" researcher Ian Stevenson.

peculiar dizziness and vertigo which came upon him with increasing frequency.

When seized with these attacks he felt that walls and buildings would fall and crush him; an extreme nausea accompanied these sensations, and if seated, he would fall forward with his head below his knees and for some time would be unable to straighten himself without help.

Unable to find any physical cause for his distress, the possibility of spirit interference was suggested, and we concentrated for him at our psychic circle.

A spirit then controlled Mrs. Wickland and fell forward with head between the knees.

We labored with the entity for some time until he was finally able to tell us that his name was Jack Finch, that he was about sixty-five years old and had been an inmate of an institution near Madison, Wisconsin.

He said that when he was quite small someone, probably his sister, had been carrying him and had dropped him to the floor and that this fall had broken his back and left him helpless. As he grew older he became a great care; his mother neglected him and he was finally placed in an institution. He remembered he had been in a cyclone at one time and that something had struck him on the back of the neck, adding still further to his misery.

He had always been in great pain, and his broken back and injured neck produced dizzy spells which would cause him to double over and remain in a cramped position until aid was given. When this dizziness came upon him he would feel as if he were sliding off a roof, or as if the walls were crushing him; again, he often felt as if the bed would fall on him and as if everything were spinning around.

He said that because of his helpless condition no one had ever cared for him, with the single exception of a nurse by the name of "Anasteena," who had been very kind to him at the institution and had always fed him.

"But everything is changed now. Sometimes I feel like a small man, and sometimes like a woman, or like a big man." (Sensations experienced when influencing different mortals.)

When the spirit was brought to a realization that he had lost his mortal body and could no longer have any physical pain, he asked: "If I have lost my body, and if I am dead, then why haven't I seen God? Where is He?"

This led to an explanation of the true nature of God, His manifestation in all things, and the existence of the spirit world.

Being told to look about to see whether someone was present whom he had known on Earth, he said: "Why, there is my mother! She wants me to go with her to her home; she says she will take care of me now. She says I never knew what real life was on account of my crippled body, but that I will commence to really live from now on."

While speaking, he saw in the distance another spirit coming toward him, and he exclaimed with great joy: "It is Anasteena! Can I go with her, too?"

Assured that he could go with his mother and friend, that he would be well cared for, and would begin a life of happiness, he said fervently, "God bless you!" and was then taken away.

The next day the friend who had suffered from the vertigo attacks found himself free from the ailment and said he had so much surplus energy that he felt he must be forty eight, instead of eighty four. Nor was he ever subject to any recurrence of his former trouble.

―――――

Mr. Z., from the neighboring town of Burbank, who had suffered for twenty-five years from sleeplessness and an intense nausea without having been able to obtain relief, was brought to us by a physician, who suspected obsession in the case.

During the consultation Mrs. Wickland saw the spirit of a man standing behind the patient, and when she described this spirit, the patient recognized an old friend who had passed out a number of years before.

After an electrical treatment had been given to the patient, this spirit left him, and taking control of Mrs. Wickland, spoke to his friend, recalling incidents of their former acquaintanceship.

"Past Life" researcher Ian Stevenson.

Mr. Z. had at one time been engaged to the daughter of this spirit, but for religious reasons the engagement had been broken. The two men had, however, continued friendly relations and when the father found himself in financial straits, Mr. Z. had aided him in a business way.

When the father later died of cancer of the stomach, he was attracted to Mr. Z. Because of his regard for him; becoming enclosed in his aura, he was unable to free himself and had remained with him for twenty-five years, conveying to his mortal friend the symptoms of the disease from which he had suffered while in Earth life.

After receiving an explanation of the laws of the higher life he left repentantly, and Mr. Z. was no longer troubled with the nausea condition.

An unusual type of psychic invalidism, due to spirit influence, was the case of Mrs. G., who had for many years suffered intensely from a peculiar spinal affliction, which baffled all skill of physicians.

After Mrs. G. had been under our care for some time a spirit who had died of a broken back and neck was removed and controlled Mrs. Wickland.

The guiding intelligences explained that he had drifted into the aura of the patient when she was a child and had become enmeshed in her nervous system, thus transferring to his victim the physical condition under which he had died, and which he still believed himself to be suffering from.

With the removal of the spirit the patient was promptly relieved and suffered no more pain in the back.[52]

What we see in these cases is that physical ailments can be caused by an attached entity, and cured by removing that entity. While I do not have a specific case of a birthmark to include here, I doubt that it would be any different, if that birthmark can be determined to be related to the attached spirit. Particularly in view of the curious case of stigmata, where living mortals have wounds on their hands or elsewhere that

---

[52] From Chapter IX of *"30 Years among the Dead"*

they believe to be the wounds of Jesus – no one ever seriously suggests these folks are reincarnations of Jesus. Even more curious is most of these are in the palms; as is the classical depiction in paintings, yet researchers now believe that Jesus was nailed through the wrists.

In this chapter we have looked at the work of the leading researcher Ian Stevenson into "past life" memories of children. He was a meticulous researcher and conclusively proved that young children could recall the details of lives that they had no way of being involved in. I think a reasonable person will accept that certainly some of these past life memories, perhaps the majority, even possibly all twenty in this book are based on real lives. But that is not sufficient evidence to conclude that reincarnation is true. What we have to prove, which is patently impossible, is that the same soul was involved. Since that is impossible, a meticulous researcher will seek to find if there is another reasonable explanation for the existence of these historic memories in the mind of a human. This we will do in later chapters.

There is one case Ian Stevenson detailed where quite clearly any conclusion about this being reincarnation falls apart because the "past" life was alive at the same time as the individual with the memory recall. There is evidence of spirit obsession in this particular case, and two other well known cases mentioned in passing. However there are the remaining cases which may in fact be subject to other causes or effects, and later in this book I will introduce other ideas which may more correctly explain how these could occur. I certainly do not hold that possession or obsession is the explanation for all past life recall.

Before leaving this book, it is useful to mention an aspect that Ian Stevenson came across infrequently, but which he nevertheless remarked on. And that is the situation where two people claim to have had the same past life. Now I have heard that explained away as a soul split, but that seems to me to be an ever more fanciful explanation of the obvious flaw in the reincarnation belief. Certainly I have not come across that suggestion from the spirit side, in fact quite the opposite – our souls are created by God, and have a long journey ahead, but there has never been any suggestion additional souls are created by splitting. And probably the only explanation that could be carried (and still remain supportive of a belief in reincarnation) is that one or other is fraudulent. Alternatively, it could be viewed as a serious objection to the belief. But I don't think there have been enough of these to deliver

"Past Life" researcher Ian Stevenson.

up a good case for scrutiny. Nevertheless that they exist should cause folks to wonder.

Looking into the matter of birthmarks that are thought to be related to a past life injury, I have illustrated that obsessing spirits can cause real physical ailments in the mortal body, which suggests to me that birthmarks could follow the same process. However I also have an alternative hypothesis that I will explore in a later chapter, rather than suggesting the birthmark comes from the past life, I will be suggesting it may be the other way around.

Chapter 6

The Law of Attraction.

As a result of the books published by Ester and Jerry Hicks, and also the best seller "The Secret"[53], many folks have become familiar with the Law of Attraction. You may be wondering what this has to do with reincarnation? The very popular book "The Law of Attraction"[54] pretty much states that everything that happens to us is brought about by the Law of Attraction. I must admit that although I personally have experienced the manifestation of just the right book within hours if not days, a number of times in the last ten years, I am still not sure if I accept everything is a result of this Law. But I do see that it is a very major factor in our lives. We are definitely creators either consciously or by default.

However, the more one studies the realm we go to after death, and which is discussed in detail in Chapter 16, the more it appears that the Law of Attraction is the absolutely dominant force in that realm. So much so, that the will of a spirit is not sufficient to overturn the judgment delivered by the Law of Attraction. But I wonder if it is the totally dominant force in this Earth realm? Still, it's definitely a significant force. While reading that book I found the opinion of Abraham on the matter of past life influence very interesting. In essence he (really the group called Abraham) says that past lives have no influence on this life, unless the mortal has obtained information about a past life, and by the power of his or her thought is giving it power in this life. I will quote here the answer given on page 95:

> "**Abraham:** You are a continually expanding Being, and your *Inner Being* is the culmination of all that you have lived. Your *Inner Being* not only believes, but knows, the worthiness and value of your Being, so as you choose thoughts that are in agreement with those of

---
[53] *The Secret* by Rhonda Byrne published byAtria Books/Beyond Words 2006.
[54] *The Law of Attraction* by Esther and Jerry Hicks, published in 2006 by Hay House, ISBN 1-4019-1227-3

> your *Inner Being*, you feel the clarity of that knowledge, however, the details of any past physical experience do not affect you in this physical experience. There is much confusion about that, and it comes largely because there are those who do not want to accept that they are the creator of their own experience. They say, "I'm fat in this life experience because I starved to death in the last." And we say: *There is nothing from past-life experience that is influencing that which you are doing now, unless, in some way, you become aware of it and are now giving it your attention.*"[55]

That struck me as curious from two respects. Firstly it truly did not sound like what I would have expected to hear from discarnates who appear to believe in reincarnation. (I would have to study a lot more Abraham material to get more clarity on that aspect, and right now that is not feasible, as the web site is not a free repository of all the Abraham material. But I do realize that spirit communication always comes through a mortal mind, and it's entirely possible that the belief in reincarnation is Esther's not Abraham's.)

Secondly, and far more importantly, it really suggests that Karma as the term is classically used is totally non-existent. Because Karma is supposed to flow from your past life mistakes, and we are supposed to carry that into this life, even if we carry no memory of previous lives. This quotation however certainly refutes that any Karma from a prior life is a factor in our current Earth life. The entire philosophic framework of classic reincarnation is that you create yourself, and have another life to improve on the results. If you do a poor job, you start at a lower point in the next life, because you are carrying the results of error.

Now saying there is no Karma is actually a very big deal, because it also suggests that there is no outcome, or result, from choosing error. Yet it's self evident that there is. As an example someone who is a drug abuser, vibrates at a very low level, with very negative energy, and is still like that after death. In fact after death such a person is what we would call a dark entity, as the results of those choices come home to manifest in the appearance of the individual. That is the direct result of

---

[55] *The Law of Attraction* page 95.

choosing unwisely. It does not go away because you are dead. Yet if one suggests that same person can reincarnate with a clean slate, there is something quite unreal about the whole philosophic framework.

Abraham also suggests, but does not say so explicitly, that there is no such thing as compensation for error. I draw that conclusion from another quotation, when asked about evil, he defines evil as that which another might do, which you would not.[56] Very much inferring that these are just choices, and no consequences flow from those choices. Again that completely contradicts what I would say I know about life after death.

In the next realm folks have to contend with the Law of Attraction acting on the soul condition that they have after death. And if there is nothing that is evil, then an awful lot of folks are having a very unhappy experience for no reason at all. Again, perhaps if I read a lot more on Abraham's views, I might discover that it is his opinion that folks are choosing darkness, and unhappiness after death. Yet the feedback from such folks is contrary to that. They do accept they were bad, and they cannot get themselves out of darkness without actually changing themselves, which certainly is at the thought level of existence. In that respect their experience is absolutely caused by their thoughts, precisely what Abraham is saying. Except he appears to believe that there is neither good nor evil. However, he certainly says that we should always note the emotion that we derive from our Inner Spirit, and only follow those actions which result in positive emotions. As I have said, I don't know enough about the full scope of Abraham's teachings to put what appear to be contradictory comments into proper perspective.

However there is another reason why I am so interested in the Law of Attraction. I was already aware that this is the fundamental Law in the realm we go to after death, because that is what was channeled by James Padgett a long time before Abraham came along. On May 29th, 1916 he channeled a message from Apostle John where he discusses what happens after death:

> *Then there comes a time, when every soul must stand alone, and in its weakness or strength realize that no*

---

[56] *Law of Attraction* page 113.

> *other soul can bear its sorrow or take from its burdens or enter into its sufferings, And thus is realized the saying that each soul is its own keeper and alone responsible for its own condition.*
>
> *Of course in many cases the loving friends may visit that soul in its place of existence and offer consolation and help and encouragement and instruction, but in some cases this cannot be, for as this soul is then laid bare to itself, all its deformities, and sins and evil qualities come before it, and thus throws around it a wall, as it were, that prevents the good friends and loving ones from appearing to it.*
>
> *And thus again comes into operation the great law of attraction for while these more elevated friends, cannot come to that soul, yet other spirits of like souls and qualities may become its associates, and render such assistance as the blind can lead the blind in their movings about.*
>
> *And I wish here to say, notwithstanding what some of your spiritualistic teachers have said, for the soul has its location as well as its condition.*[57]

It is further channeled within the Padgett Messages that the Law of Attraction is what draws to a living mortal either advanced (discarnate) loving guides and teachers, or evil, un-evolved dark entities seeking to indulge in their still active material desires. So I am quite comfortable with how the universe supports the thoughts of the living mortal, without really judging. If your desires are spiritually advanced, you get that support, and if your desires are materially base, they too are supported. That however should never be interpreted as suggesting there are no implications for choosing unwisely.

Which brings us to the practice of past life regression. There are today many hypnotherapists offering to assist folks by regressing them to a "past life". One of the more popular of these is Brian Weiss[58], and he has described the results his patients achieve. On the face of it, surely the fact that he can hypnotize folks, and get information that directly relates to their current life, and frequently results in a substantial re-

---

[57] https://new-birth.net/link7/ received by James Padgett on May 29th, 1916
[58] *Same Soul, Many Bodies: Discover the Healing Power of Future Lives through Progression Therapy* by Brian Weiss

The Law of Attraction.

assessment of that current life leads great credence to the notion of reincarnation? Yes, on the surface I am sure that is so. But let's look a little bit deeper into what is happening, in my view.

The purpose of the regression session is healing, and this is clear to both the hypnotherapist and the patient. So the Universe is quite clear on the objective. Hypnotism is utilized, which makes the patient a good medium, and in almost all cases a past life experience is found, possibly many such past lives. In the case of Dr Weiss, these not only relate directly to the circumstances of the patient, but all too frequently the patient will report that they were able to recognize someone who is a key player in their current drama, in that past life event. That set of historic events very frequently seems to explain, or clarify what is occurring in the current life. It is as if the patient is able to take a very objective look at themselves, in another setting, and with a different drama, but sufficient commonality to see what is happening and draw very useful conclusions about the current life.

In short it is a wonderful means of diagnosis and healing, and I certainly think it has great value. The only problem I can see, is that I am sure the past life event is selected precisely because it is a good match for the current life, and this is where the Law of Attraction plays its part. So what I am saying is that instead of believing that the patient committed those historic acts, the patient should view this as a more objective explanation of their own life than they probably currently have. Even the issue of birth marks I am sure can happen that way, as also the issue of recognizing key players. Because there is a search for meaning, the Law of Attraction can match up all these things – in fact anything that you give priority to, including the current players in the real life, and find a past life from the billions that have occurred, and which is going to be a good diagnostic. In short the Law of Attraction does exactly what Esther and Jerry Hicks say it can do in finding a real past life for the curious that will be most effective in achieving healing in the now.

Of course it is certainly not the case that every reported past life is a perfect match for this life's troubles. It is probably only when the intention is to heal the problems of this life that this occurs.

In short what I am suggesting is that the search for healing causes the Law of Attraction to deliver up a past life memory, and not the other way around. This is probably a rather radical suggestion for most folks to consider, and it also surprises me in that I have not previously found such a simple explanation for the perfect fit between the current life and the diagnostic past life.

Chapter 7

Trying to Reincarnate.

The young lad "Lionel" was mentioned earlier as looking up to David Hatch, in "Letters from a living dead man."[59] This lad adopts the Judge as a mentor, and spends considerable time in his adult company. Lionel is really keen to reincarnate, and eventually announces he has chosen his new mother and father, that she is pregnant, and Lionel disappears to be "reincarnated". We hear no more about Lionel. The book "Letters from a living dead man" only covers approximately a year, and Lionel does not reappear. One for the opposition you may shout, surely that proves reincarnation is possible?

I agree it is a great pity that Lionel did not reappear in the book. If indeed I were capable of it, I would be looking out for either Lionel or David Hatch right now, and attempting to see if he will communicate. As it is a good 104 years since 1912, it is time for Lionel to be back in spirit, supposing he did manage to reincarnate, and had a normal lifespan. However I suspect he will have a very different story to tell and I will take you there courtesy of another hypnotherapist, Dr Irene Hickman and another psychic researcher, Dr. Carl Wickland. Hearing it from Lionel would be better though. That would be a real coup. But after initial publication in 2011, I came across another fascinating book, where the spirit actually raises this topic. This is Karen, as reported by her mother Jeanne Walker.[60]

Dr Irene Hickman was also a believer in reincarnation. She has passed on sadly, because I truly would have loved to have chatted to her, but we have heard from her in spirit, courtesy of a friend of mine. Amazingly, she says she has moved on from her belief in reincarnation. I was truly surprised to hear that. She wrote an amazing book – "Remote Depossession."[61] In this book she explains how in her practice

---

[59] Letter 11 of "Letters from a living dead man."
[60] "More Alive Than Ever"...Always, Karen. By Jeanne Walker.
[61] Remote Depossession, Dr Irene Hickman, published by Hickman Systems 1994. ISBN 0-915689-08-1 This may prove hard to purchase for a reasonable price, and contact details are provided at the end of this book.

Is Reincarnation an Illusion?

as a hypnotherapist she discovers that many people have attached spirit entities. While some of these seem to be of non-human origin, she also frequently finds ex-mortals attached. This may be a distasteful subject to those who have never considered that this may be a possibility.

I will first quote from her book a typical spirit releasement procedure, and then I will look at the two cases that are relevant to Lionel. But before going into that detail I would like to comment that I do not think that Lionel is typical of spirits who "want to reincarnate," although his is not the only case I have come across. In his case he simply returns to the Earth plane, having chosen his mom, and knowing that she is pregnant. Even though I am not a believer in reincarnation, it sounds far too simplistic, indeed, even childlike. The point I would like to address, is what might have become of Lionel? And, in talking about this, I will have another opportunity to address the topic of past life memories from a slightly different perspective.

As this extract is simply taken from Chapter 8 in the middle of "Remote Depossession," I should explain the method. Dr. Irene Hickman, as a trained professional hypnotherapist, hypnotises an assistant. This assistant, called a subject below, becomes effectively a medium, and is able to be used by Irene; to interact with the patient and any attached spirits. The patient is most often not aware that this procedure is being conducted, and may be remote, indeed even across the world, but the patient's higher consciousness is always asked for permission. The beauty of this approach is that reports of improvement are quite independent, as the patient most often has no idea what has transpired, because typically it is a concerned relative who has asked for this healing approach. It is also totally non-invasive, unlike some reports of traditional church procedures. Just to make it totally clear, the patient, or the person with the problem, is generally not in the same room with Irene Hickman, and has most often no idea the procedure is going to be performed.

Sample Remote Depossession Session, Chicago, IL. March 1993.

The hypnotized subject was Rhona, a participant in a two-day seminar. I, Dr. Irene Hickman, conducted the session. We were asked to scan Marion's (not her real name)

Trying to reincarnate.

mother, Joan, in Paris, France, at a specific address. Joan was located by sending a bit of Rhona's consciousness to the address in Paris. Permission to scan Joan was requested from Joan's higher self. Permission was granted somewhat reluctantly after we explained that our purpose was to help Joan and intended no harm.

Dr. H. Begin scanning Joan. Tell me what you find.
Rhona. There is a darkness in both arms and the solar plexus.
Dr. H. Anything else?
Rhona. Behind her in her aura.
Dr. H. What else?
Rhona. Something jumping up and down on the top of her head.
Dr H. Anything else?
Rhona. That's all.
Dr. H. I call to you in the arms of Joan, Marions' mother to come forward, speak through Rhona without harming her in any way or give her your thoughts so she can speak for you and identify yourself. Do you have a name?
(Asking for a name is intended to determine whether this is one who formerly had their own body or is one from the darkness.)
Rhona. Pierre.
Dr H. What happened to your body Pierre? (Response was so slow that it raised doubts as to the entities true nature.) Did you really have a body?
Pierre. Yes
Dr. H. Tell me what happened to it.
Pierre. I drank some poison from a cup.
Dr. H. Then what happened to your body?
Pierre. My body is there on the floor.
Dr. H. Then what did you do?
Pierre. I just waited until someone came along.
Dr. H. When this person came along, what happened?
Pierre. This person. She was kind.
Dr. H. How old was Joan when you joined her?
Pierre. Eight.

Is Reincarnation an Illusion?

Dr. H. Do you know that you are having a detrimental effect on Joan, and that you are holding back your own development? How do you feel about that?
Pierre. There's nothing else.
Dr. H. If there is a better place, are you interested?
Pierre. I suppose so.
Dr. H. There is a place, called "The Light" - a place for us to go when our body dies. It is much pleasanter than staying attached to Joan. In this place you grow and learn and eventually come back in a new body of your own. Would you like to have your own body again?
Pierre. Yes.
Dr. H. I call on anyone in "The Light" who cares about Pierre to come for him and greet him, communicate with him and help him with his transition. Pierre, look up and tell me what you see.
Pierre. I see my mama.
Dr. H. Communicate with her. Ask her what it is like there. What does she tell you?
Pierre. She says it's a good place.
Dr. H. Do you think that might be better than staying with Joan?
Pierre. Yes.
Dr. H. Then get ready to join your mama. But first I ask something of you. I would like you to look around inside Joan's body and around the periphery for any other beings that are lost and confused and are attached to Joan's body as you have been. You have a chance to gather them up and take them with you to this good place. Call to them. Are they coming?
Pierre. The one in the other arm is coming.
Dr. H. Are the others coming?
Pierre. The one in the abdomen is coming.
Dr H. And the one jumping up and down on the top of Joan's head. Is that one of your nature or of a different nature?
Pierre. That one's not like me.

Trying to reincarnate.

Dr. H.   We will come back and check that one later. Take your mother's hand and the hands of those who are willing to go with you. Go in peace with our love and blessing. Thank you so much, Pierre, for helping. Now I ask the healing angels to fill with healing light the areas just vacated by those who have departed.
Now you, who are jumping up and down on Joan's head, come forward, speak through Rhonda without harming her in any way and identify yourself. Do you have a name?

Entity.   No.

Dr. H.   Have you ever had a name?

Entity.   No.

Dr. H.   Have you ever had your own human physical body?

Entity.   No.

Dr. H.   I call now on the Forces of St Michael to come with a net of Light, and wrap it around all of the dark beings in or around the being of Joan. Pull the net snug and keep tightening it slowly but steadily until these beings respond to my questions promptly and truthfully. Speak through Rhona without harming her in any way, or give her your thoughts. What is your purpose here in Joan?

Entity.   To make her miserable.

Dr. H.   You've done a good job of that haven't you?

Entity.   Yes.

Dr. H.   How old was Joan when you joined her?

Entity.   Thirty.

Dr. H.   Were you given an order to make her miserable?

Entity.   No.

Dr. H.   I want a truthful answer. (No response.) Do you take orders from any being? Were you given instructions before you came to Joan?

Entity.   Hmmmmm.

Dr. H.   When you were given instructions, what were you told about Light?

Entity.   I was told to avoid it.

Is Reincarnation an Illusion?

Dr. H. What is the reason you were given for avoiding Light?
Entity. It would make me disappear.
Dr. H. That isn't true and I will show you. I ask now that the Forces of St Michael send a shaft of light through this "dark" one. And another and another and another. Did you disappear? Did it hurt you?
Entity. No, no.
Dr. H. You have been lied to. You have been deceived. The one who gave you your orders was wrong. Are you willing to continue taking instructions and orders from one who lies and deceives?
Entity. I would like to try that other thing.
Dr. H. You've heard about the other place? Have you been watching what we have been doing here today?
Entity. Yes.
Dr. H. What do you think about what we have been doing?
Entity. It's dangerous.
Dr. H. Dangerous in what way?
Entity. I might get into trouble.
Dr. H. You were told to stay hidden too weren't you?
Entity. Unhumm
Dr. H. Now you've been found. What happens to beings like you who don't stay hidden?
Entity. It's not good.
Dr. H. Have you been to that place of punishment before?
Entity. Yes.
Dr. H. What kind of place is it?
Entity. Pain, cold, lonely.
Dr. H. Now that you have been found, there is a chance that you will be sent there again. Would you like that? (Although some "dark" entities deny ever having been to a place of punishment - the Pit - they all admit knowing about it and that it is most unpleasant. Fear of punishment seems to be the primary motivation for following orders of their bosses.)

Trying to reincarnate.

Entity. No. It's bad.
Dr. H. Fortunately you do have another option. Those beings that have enclosed you in the net have come to rescue you and take you home. Some of them were once like you. Look at them now. How do they look?
Entity. They are bright.
Dr. H. How would you like to be more like them? (No response.) You may communicate with them. Ask them if they ever had a job of causing pain and misery. Ask them what their existence is like now.
Entity. They say it's good.
Dr. H. And they don't have to worry about being sent to that awful place. Do you think you would like to go with them?
Entity. Yes.
Dr. H. In order to get ready to go, there is something you must do. Look deep within the centre of your being and tell me what you see there.
Entity. A little speck of light.
Dr. H. Watch that little speck. What happens as you watch?
Entity. It's getting bigger and brighter. (Tone of surprise.)
Dr. H. Keep watching. Now what's happening?
Entity. It keeps growing.
Dr. H. That bit of light was there all the time, but you didn't know it. All it takes for it to grow is for you to recognise it. What's happening to your darkness?
Entity. It's gone.
Dr. H. The others in and around Joan have been watching what has happened to you. Tell them to look to the centres of their being. Tell me what they are finding at their centres.
Entity. They are changing too.
Dr. H. You were all operating from fear. Now you have another way to function. Are all of the former "dark" ones ready to go now?
Entity. Yes.

67

Is Reincarnation an Illusion?

Dr. H.   Fine. Go in peace with our love and blessing. As you leave Joan's body, call out through the universe for all beings of your former "dark" nature to come and follow. Call out to all of equal rank and stature, of lesser rank and stature, and of greater rank and stature. Even call to your commander. That one might come too. Call out. Are you calling?

Entity.   Yes.

Dr. H.   Are they coming?

Entity.   Yes.

Dr. H.   How many?

Entity.   319.

Dr. H.   Ask each one to look inside and find their true nature at their core. Thank you for helping. I now call on the healing angels to come and fill with healing light all the spaces in and around Joan's body that were vacated by those beings who just left. Rhona, once again scan Joan. Are there any other areas where there is need for more of this kind of work.

Rhona.   Around her ankles.

Dr H.   You in Joan's ankles, come forward, speak through Rhona without harming her in anyway and identify yourself. Do you have a name?

Entity.   Lois.

Dr. H.   Tell me about yourself, Lois. With a name you must have had your own physical body. What happened to that body?

Lois.   Hit by a car. I fell out the door.

Dr. H.   How old were you when this happened?

Lois.   Ten.

Dr. H.   Then what happened? The car hit your body, but what happened to you?

Lois.   There was a lady there.

Dr. H.   Did you know this lady?

Lois.   I didn't know what to do. I went with her.

Dr. H.   This is not your body. You're in someone else's body. There is a much better place for you to be. It's called "The Light." Would you like to know about this place?

Trying to reincarnate.

Lois.   I think so.

Dr. H.   I call now on anyone in "The Light" who cares about Lois to come for her, greet her, show themselves to her, communicate with her and help her transition. Lois look up and tell me what you see.

Lois.   My sister.

Dr. H.   I would like you to ask your sister what it's like where she is. What does she tell you?

Lois.   It's nice.

Dr. H.   Prepare to go, but before you do, please look around to see if there are any others who are attached as you have been because they did not go to "The Light."

Lois.   No others.

Dr. H.   Fine, then go in peace with our love and blessing. Goodbye Lois. Again I ask the healing angels to fill the space vacated by Lois, Rhona, scan Joan again. Are there more?

Rhona. No.

Dr. H.   Fine, now look at the very centre of Joan. Find the brightest point of her spirit, focus on it and watch it expand to fill her body. Tell me when her body is completely filled with Light or if you encounter any areas that fail to fill.

Rhona. She's filled.

Dr. H.   Now let the Light expand beyond her body at least arm's length in all directions until she is completely enclosed in a bubble or cocoon of Light comforting, strengthening and protecting her. Tell me when this is complete.

Rhona. It's complete.

Dr. H.   Then bring that bit of your consciousness back from Paris, back to Chicago, to this room and to your body.

Rhona. There's something on my left shoulder.

Dr. H.   You on Rhona's left shoulder, come forward, speak through Rhona's voice without harming her in any way and identify yourself. Do you have a name?

Entity. Samuel.

Is Reincarnation an Illusion?

Dr. H. Samuel, what are you doing here on Rhona's shoulder?
Samuel. I was with Joan. I didn't go. (This is the only time this has happened in my experience.)
Dr. H. You must have had a good reason for not wanting to go. What is the reason?
Samuel. I just didn't want to go.
Dr. H. You may have missed a wonderful opportunity. Those who come from "The Light" to greet their loved ones all say it's wonderful there. Is it wonderful where you are?
Samuel. It's not easy here.
Dr. H. Are you telling me that you can't stick to Rhona very easily?
Samuel. Right.
Dr. H. I now call on anyone in "The Light" who cares about Samuel to come for him, greet him, communicate with him and help him with his transition. Samuel, look up. Tell me what you see.
Samuel. My girlfriend Louise.
Dr. H. Do you want to stay here on Rhona's shoulder or do you want to go with Louise?
Samuel. I'll go.
Dr. H. That wasn't a very difficult decision then?
Samuel. No.
Dr. H. Then go in peace with our love and blessing. Join Louise. I ask now for the healing angels to come and fill the spaces with Light that were just vacated by Samuel. Rhona, is there anything else we need to do for you?
Rhona. No more.
Dr. H. Then focus on the centre of your being and find the brightest point of your spirit. Let this brightness fill your body and extend beyond forming a great cocoon of Light around you.
Rhona. It's formed.
Dr. H. Prepare to waken. The forces within your body will equalise. I will soon waken you by counting

Trying to reincarnate.

> *backward from twenty-one to one using alternate figures.*[62]

Now that you have an idea of the technique, I will refer to two short case studies that are perhaps a bit closer to the situation I believe Lionel may have found himself in.

> *We then inquired of Dee's inner Wisdom – "is it appropriate for Dee to scan Richard A. in Palo Alto?" Approval was granted. Dee was able to locate Richard and receive his high self permission to scan him for the possible presence of attached entities.*
>
> *Dee located dark areas in Richard's navel, lower internal organs and genitals. I asked the entity to come forward and identify itself. No response. Then Dee said, "It's a little girl. She's not good at language. She had a great desire to be Richard's child and stayed in his reproductive organs hoping Richard would give her the seed of life."*
>
> Dr. H.   *Little girl, do you know about "The Light" – a place to rest and learn while waiting for a new body?*
> Girl.   *What is "the Light?"*
> Dr. H.   *It's a wonderful place of preparation for a new body. You will be doing much better by going to this place rather than staying here in a body that is not your own.*
> Girl.   *Can I have a mom?*
> Dr. H.   *I call now on anyone in "The Light" who cares about this little girl in the body of Richard, to come for her, greet her, communicate with her and help her move to "The Light."*
> Girl.   *Yes! Mom! (She left at once.)*
> Dr. H.   *I call now for the healing angels to bring Light to fill the space where the little girl was. (Dee began to shake her head.) What is it?*
> Dee.   *The little girl wants us to tell Richard that she is OK, that he doesn't have to wait for her or work for her or hope for her at any level, and*

---

[62] *Remote Depossession*, Chapter 8 pages 72-83.

Is Reincarnation an Illusion?

	he is not to worry. I agreed that we would let him know. Then Dee began to fill Richard's body with Light, shaking her head all the while.
Dr. H.	*What is it?*
Dee.	*He needs a different diet that is clean and clear and not contaminated, that has not had a lot of processing and handled by people who don't care.*
Dr. H.	*Has "The Light" filled Richard completely?*
Dee.	*Yes, and it extends around him in a bubble.*[63]

In this tale we see a young girl hoping to be born. One could assume that she was an "Earthbound" spirit, but we don't know that for sure. Earthbound spirits have not yet reached the Spirit Spheres – also called "The Light." They fail to transition, after death, and are found in the Astral Planes, most commonly in the Earth plane. In some cases they can also return to the Earth Plane immediately after initially transitioning. They need not "attach" to another mortal, they can also simply be found in homes and other places on Earth – ghosts is what we probably mostly call them. Although there are also ghosts that are without a soul, that are simply energetic signatures, and cannot be conversed with. This topic is covered in Chapter 16.

In Lionel's case, he was in the Astral Plane. This much is clear from the context of the book. Normally, as Lionel is a young fellow, I would expect that he would have been in the upper First Sphere, because children are not found any lower than "Summerland." While one might expect that Lionel should be in a specific place in the next realms, clearly he is one of those children who do not "pass over" correctly. I will now quote some other examples from "Remote Depossession."

> *This case, sent to me by Scott Herner of Scandia, Minnesota, concerns a young girl who had for four years manifested both behaviour and health problems. The remote depossession was requested by her mother. Mother reported that before the sudden change, Erin had been very pleasant, bright, happy, and intelligent and always getting along with her sisters. She had at about five, begun to talk of having been abused, but could recall*

---

[63] *Remote Depossession*, pages 140-141.

Trying to reincarnate.

no details of the abuse. At age seven, Erin developed headaches located from the top of her head down the left side.

The changed pattern of behavior included vehement non-cooperation, obnoxiousness and being annoying and mean to her younger sister, even hitting her at times.

Scott, with the assistance of an associate, Dodo S. located three Earthbound entities in Erin. The one in the head appeared to have tentacles going down the left side of her head. This one was Jim. Jim had died in the hospital and had joined Erin when she was being treated in the same hospital for a broken leg. Jim's presence was causing headaches and her abhorrent behavior. Jim's father came for him in "The Light" but before Jim left he mentioned Agnes, in Erin's shoulder. Agnes had fallen outside on a cold day and had died before anyone found her. She had joined Erin for lack of a better place to go. Jim also named the one in Erin's left leg. This was Joe who refused to go to "The Light" with him. Agnes left with her sister, Lenore who came for her.

After Jim had left with his father and Agnes with her sister, Lenore, Scott dialoged with Joe. Joe petulantly stated that he "wasn't going anywhere." Further questioning brought the response that he had been very badly abused while very young and had been beaten to death when he was four. He commented that he didn't think it was fair to die at such a young age. He had joined Erin when she was five. Scott told Joe about "The Light" and that he could have his own body there. When the call was made for anyone in "The Light" to come for Joe, Grandma Annie came. Then Joe was willing to go.

Erin's body was filled and surrounded with light. The very next morning, Erin was a changed child. She even told her mother that she felt different. She is much happier and quieter. This report was sent about five weeks after the depossession. During these five weeks the new attitude and behavior had continued. She gets along well with her sisters with no more hitting. Her aunt also remarked about the marked change in Erin.

The most significant part of this, I feel, is that Joe, who had been abused and beaten to death at four, had joined

Is Reincarnation an Illusion?

> *Erin when she was five. Erin began at that time to talk of being abused herself without being able to come up with any pertinent details. This raises the question as to whether other children may have felt abused because of an attached entity rather than from their own personal abuse. Could this be the reason for what has been called false memory syndrome?*[64]

Well this story raises a few very interesting issues. Not simply the issue of how Erin managed to gain the memories from the mind of an attached spirit, but also the issue of how attached spirits can manifest physical symptoms in Erin, and affect her mental and emotional balance. So often in "past life" recalls, we see cases of reported explanations for current physical or emotional problems. Are these being explained by memories long past, or are they caused by currently attached spirits? We won't know until a lot more research is done. Only one case was reported by Irene Hickman of an attached spirit that claimed to be very old. Indeed that spirit claimed to have lived in a previous life with the mortal. That was something that I found difficult to believe, simply because it suggested it had remained attached all that time, and I have only once read of attachments in the Spirit Spheres, as opposed to here, in the Earth plane. We do need to allow for spirits to be confused, and even deluded, just as mortals can be. The case of spirit attachment, which continued in the Spirit Spheres, is reported in "Life Here and Hereafter" by Charlotte Elizabeth Dresser. This book specifically deals with a mortal working with a number of spirits to assist folks to pass over, and deals with many recalcitrant recently departed folks.

All of this raises the issue of "where is the mind?" Something we started to address in Chapter 3. Perhaps I should say: "Local mind," since folks also talk of an Akashic Field, or Akashic Record, which appears to be a shared repository. In yet another fabulous book, "Love without End"[65], Glenda Green quotes Jesus as saying our mind resides outside, and around the body, in a magnetic, and digital state. This is a book well worth reading. But if the mind is external, in what way, is it associated with the aura? I suspect it may be the same thing, or a part

---
[64] *Remote Depossession*, pages 150-152.
[65] *Love without End*, by Glenda Green, published by Spiritis Publishing, 1999, ISBN 0-9666623-1-8

Trying to reincarnate.

of that, because of an interesting explanation given in "Astral Travel". Here we read:

> *If you are embarrassed by nudity when you astral project you should remember to clothe the astral body. To do this, the only thing necessary is to think yourself into clothing, and magically your astral body will be attired. That clothing will not conceal your emotional attributes. If you are a negative or unpleasant or hateful person, those characteristics will show through whatever guise you assume on the astral. When you physically change your appearance from that of, say, a young person to someone old, still your habitual emotions will be visible to other astral entities. There is no hiding of emotion on the astral. Therefore the first thing you should do when you get on to the astral is to find a way of seeing yourself. For this purpose a normal mirror does not work, because it does not reflect astral attributes. What you need instead is a pool of spring water. If you can find a spring overhung by trees and therefore dark, that is ideal for your purpose. The spring is a place you will visit many times as you develop; so once you have found it, you should memorise it's location.*
>
> *Look at yourself closely in the calm surface of the water. Think of something on the physical plane that makes you angry. Now look at yourself again in your spring-fed mirror of truth. See how you have changed? See how the flow around you has become suffused with the deep reds of hate? Think now of something pleasant and spiritual. Look again into your mirror and see how much improved you have become.*[66]

That little experiment illustrates that the colours surrounding the spirit body change as the thoughts of the spirit change. That sounds exactly like the aura to me, and pretty much confirms it is a representation of the mind. It would not surprise me to discover that the aura is simply the mind. (To those who have not come across a "thought form" before, the clothing that spirits wear is simply that, a thought form - a creation brought about by will.)

---

[66] *Astral Travel*, page 59.

Is Reincarnation an Illusion?

This story about auras does remind me of a time when I had my aura "cleaned," and I must say I felt a lot better after it. I was also told that auras can be damaged by things like operations, and need to be repaired. I think that there may be a lot in that, and it is surprising how often Irene Hickman found attached spirits that had initially attached in hospital. And if you read the first case study carefully, you may have noticed that Samuel could not "stick" to Rhona easily. Presumably Rhona had a nice shiney aura. But the reason why I introduced these few passages is if the mind and aura are one, attached spirits are "inside" the aura, and well within the mind area. Hence easy to confuse their memories and thoughts with our own.

Back to little Erin. Does Erin read the mind of the attached spirit, or does the attached spirit place its memories in her mind? One can't be certain, but given that Erin is so vague about her "abuse," I tend to suspect it is Erin reading the attached entity's mind, which is probably even in the very same area physically – if we can use that word when talking about other dimensions. If Erin were hypnotised, I rather suspect her memory recall would be better.

Another interesting issue is how our consciousness can travel, yet something remains localized because the subject continues to talk. This is not unlike the effect realized with a new technique called "co-ordinate remote viewing." This technique is well described by Courtney Brown, in "Cosmic Voyage."[67] A very similar thing occurs, where the viewer is able to obtain remote information, yet write down his impressions where the body remains. A sort of two places at once OBE. (out-of-body experience) The really interesting thing about Courtney Browne's book is that this technique can be validated, simply because many of the chosen targets are on Earth. The remote viewer generally does not know what the target is, as it is simply a set of co-ordinates, but of course the controller knows. And subsequently, the results can be compared. So this book proves that we can travel with our mind and obtain accurate data.

In fact, although some might find "Cosmic Voyage" a little too farfetched with its stories of aliens, some of the items are definitely

---

[67] *Cosmic Voyage*, by Courtney Brown, published by the Penguin Group, 1997. ISBN 0-451-19026-2

Trying to reincarnate.

real. For example Courtney Browne confirms the existence of midwayers, the very same beings my friend George Barnard has been dealing with for 60 years. And to be honest, his (Courtney Browne) stories about aliens have a greater ring of truth than anything else I have read. Mostly I simply avoid the alien stuff, just too weird for me.

As an aside, after I first read Irene's book on remote depossession, I was very upset about the very large number of attached spirits who are children, even babies. As I thrashed around, angry, and searching for answers, I managed to get some answers. I am still not happy about the situation, but apparently because of the Lucifer Rebellion, and the large numbers of angels who followed him into rebellion, for many thousands of years we have simply not had enough loyal midwayers here. Midwayers are the closest spirit being to us, and they are in fact material, but we can't see them. It is their job to pack us off to the Spirit Spheres on death, but there just have not been anywhere near enough of them to keep up with the work load. As a result, those spirits that don't go to "The Light" of their own accord have been left here in limbo. Things have changed in the last ten or fifteen years in terms of the numbers of midwayers here, but there is such a big backlog, and it will take a long time to clear. It made me feel a little better, but not much.

The other thing that bothered me was how often a close spirit relative would turn up to collect the baby spirit. It seemed crazy why they can respond instantly to the call from a human, yet have never responded previously on their own initiative, or indeed not have known about the plight of the relative. The very same issue is reported quite frequently in "30 Years among the Dead."[68] It seems that the attached spirit in some way disappears from celestial radar when within the aura of a mortal.

Finally, I will now introduce a paper asserting that past life memories are caused by adjacent spirit memories, rather than being extracted from Akashic Records. In the Padgett circles, when questions have been asked concerning the source of past life memories, generally the answer seems to be that it is caused by adjacent spirit memories. I no longer am certain that this is necessarily the prime source, but as we see in the case of Erin, it certainly could be sometimes.

---

[68] *30 Years among the Dead* – Carl A. Wickland. M.D. Now out of print. Newcastle Publishing Company.

Is Reincarnation an Illusion?

One fine afternoon in the city's central park, at a New Age fair my number was called and I won the raffle. The prize was a three-hour psychic reading, compliments of the Berkeley Psychic Institute (which had a chapter in Santa Cruz at the time). I was not particularly thrilled with the prize because I thought this was nothing more than fortune telling, and I was definitely not interested in someone telling me my future - just in case they were wrong. Nevertheless, I booked the reading (probably because it was so rare that I won anything I guess I didn't want to see it go to waste).

On arriving at the Institute, I was led to a first floor room where, to my surprise, I was introduced to not one, but three psychics who were to do the reading. They seated themselves in a row, and I was told "Take the chair in front of us and try not to be nervous." The first two hours of the reading were filled with interesting and useful information about myself, my life and my future. The last hour was to be dedicated to uncovering my past lives.

In that final hour, I was told that I had had many lives. The first past life they spoke about was that of an ancient Hebrew; it was in this life that I had made a pact with God and died in His service. I must admit that I liked this very much; it not only made me feel important, it also could have been a possible explanation for my burning spiritual desire. Next, they told me that I was in the Crusades and was killed trying to free the Holy Land. From there, I lived as a Frenchman and was robbed and murdered on the road to Paris. Following that life, I was a World War I soldier killed in the trenches of Europe. After that life was revealed to me, my body began to shake. And, with each additional past life they described, the shaking intensified. I didn't know what was happening I could only think that it was my kundulini rising. Then, all of a sudden, the door swung open, and the director of the school burst into the room and exclaimed, in a huff, "What are all these spirits doing in the room? Get them out of here!" And, she began to order the psychics about, "You, open the window. You,

Trying to reincarnate.

move the chairs. You, do this; you do that. This reading is over!"

I was stunned and bewildered as well as disappointed that my reading had ended so abruptly. On the way home in the car, I kept asking myself over and over, 'What was that all about and why was the director so upset?'

As the weeks passed, I longed for answers; then, one day, they seemed to pop into my head. It was as if I was told that it was true, indeed, that there were 'spirits in the room' and they were hovering around me during the reading and it was their combined soul power that created an energy field strong enough to shake my body. It was also true that the psychics were skilled at their craft and were able to read the identities of the 'spirits in the room' and in particular their last experience on Earth their death. However, I somehow realized that their mistake was telling me that the lives they were reading were my past lives when in reality, they were the lives of the "spirits in the room."[69]

This suggestion, that psychics often read "adjacent" spirit memories, is interesting, but very hard to prove. As we have seen, it is possible to obtain memories in many ways. How would we go about identifying some as having come from adjacent spirits? I really don't know. But it is likely to be one of the causes.

"30 Years among the Dead," by Carl A. Wickland is full of transcripts like those in "Remote Depossession," but it includes a number where the spirit believes in reincarnation. Here is a transcript from page 334.

EXPERIENCE, NOVEMBER 19, 1916

Spirit: WILLIAM STANLEY   Psychic: MRS. WICKLAND

Spirit: Is it really true that I am well now? Can I talk? Can I move my arms and feet? Then reincarnation is true, because before I could neither talk nor walk. How did I get out of the child?
Doctor: Intelligent spirits brought you here for help.

---

[69] Spirits in the Room, by Alan Ross, https://new-birth.net/link18/

Is Reincarnation an Illusion?

Sp.   I wanted to come back and reincarnate in a child, and I got in and could not get out. I was so paralyzed that I could not express myself and I was in an awful state.

I was a Theosophist and I wanted to reincarnate to be great. I got into a child's body and crippled it, and also crippled my mind and that of the child. I stayed in the child because I did not know how to get out. I acted as a child and I could not talk.

I know I passed out of my mortal body some years ago, far away in India, but I do not realize when it took place. I wanted so much to reincarnate and to come back to this Earth life to live my other Karma. Do not hold on to the thought of coming back, but look for something higher, for the state I was in was the worst torture anybody could have.

I lived in Calcutta and wanted to learn to be a Master and go through my Karma, but instead I am as you see me to be.

I reincarnated in a child and became crippled, and I also got into the vibration of the mother. It was very hard and I want to warn others never to come back and try to reincarnate through a little child. Leave reincarnation alone, because it is only a mistake, but the philosophy of Theosophy is very fine.

Look upward; don't think of the astral shells, for they are of no use.

I was very selfish and wanted to come back to Earth life just to be something great, but instead I got into a very low state. I had intended to show the Theosophists that I could come back and reincarnate in a child.

Madam Blavatsky should have taught differently. (Pointing to an invisible.) I will tell you, Madam, you are the one who is to blame for the condition I am in today.

Madam Blavatsky stands here trying to help me now. She is the one who gave me the teachings and thoughts of reincarnation, and now she is trying to show me the right way and states there is no such thing as reincarnation.

Trying to reincarnate.

    One gets all mixed up trying to enter another's body for reincarnation.

Dr. What is your name?

Sp. I cannot recall my name just now.
    Madam Blavatsky was in India and taught Theosophy, had many followers and I was with her. I have also met Anna Kingsford and Dr. Hartmann, and he also was to blame for my condition.
    They pushed me in here that I might be taught and freed. I am so pleased that I can talk again; that is something I have not been able to do for years.
    Madam Blavatsky, Anna Kingsford and the Judge were all great lights, and now they have found out their big mistakes. They are all working to get their victims free, and so they brought me to this place for instruction and guidance.
    I was in India, having been there for many years. My father was an officer in the Army. I spent most of my time in Calcutta, where I met all the great lights of Theosophy, and I joined the Theosophical Society. I liked Colonel Olcott; he was a great fellow.
    I remember being very sick in India for some time. I have no desire to reincarnate again because reincarnation is a wrong doctrine. It creates a selfishness to come back.
    One can learn without being reincarnated. What I suppose did I learn in my last reincarnation in the child? What did I learn?
    I believed in Theosophy and my Karma, and I thought I had to go through with it.
    Colonel Olcott belonged to the Great Masters. He belonged to the spirit of Fire and Water — I mean the elementals of Fire and Water.

Dr. Have you ever heard of mediums?

Sp. They are only astral shells. Madam Blavatsky says we must all help those who try to reincarnate. She and the others have come to say they are trying to help and for that purpose have formed a big society. I thought I had come to life when I came here, and that I could reincarnate and talk to them as I did in life. I did not know they had passed over. Teaching

> *as they did, why did they not reincarnate the same as I?*
> *Madam Blavatsky was a great missionary, as you know. She says she is now trying to make all her victims understand about the life after this as it really is.*
> *She says that she was a medium at one time, but that she did not want anybody to control her. She thought you should develop your own self and mental faculties, and go through your Karma.*
> *I should not have been taught the falseness I was. Madam tells me that I should listen to this gentleman, (Dr. W.) and that he will explain things. Explanations were given regarding life on the Earth plane, the preparation for the life that is to follow, and the fact that the knowledge and wisdom gained here will be the light of understanding each one carries to the other side of life.*
> *The spirit finally gave the name of William Stanley, and departed, grateful for the enlightenment he had received.*[70]

There are quite a number of these experiences in this book, and it seems that it is not at all uncommon for those who believe in reincarnation to attempt this, and become caught within the magnetic aura of the mortal.

Before we move on I will quote from a spirit declaring that many an individual who is in spirit, and is determined to reincarnate, ends up obsessing a living mortal. This is from Chapter 16 of "More Alive Than Ever"...Always Karen.[71]

> *"HERE WE GO for another 'bump' up against obstructed thought.*
> *"Those who have practiced reincarnation have insisted that one has a destiny and that it is necessary to*

---

[70] *30 Years Among the Dead*, by Carl. A. Wickland, published by Newcastle Publishing Company, INC. ISBN 0-87877-025-9 (Out of print) page 334 to 336.
[71] An e-book can be obtained here: https://new-birth.net/link8/

work out one's karma on earth plane before one can go on to other planes of experience.

"Here again is one of those obstructed thoughts. We do have a kind of destiny and a kind of karma-serving our purpose and developing quantity. However, because we cannot develop more quality and serve additional purposes on earth, we limit ourselves by trying to come back and 'do it over.'

"Whatever amount of quantity we develop in one lifetime is sufficient. Repetition of earth experience isn't necessary for further development of quantity, for little is added in a second trial.

"And even more, such a belief shows a limitation of understanding of what happens in my world. Our job here is the development of greater quality. The individual who fails to take the opportunity to develop quality here because he wants to reincarnate there, not only fails himself but the purpose of evolution as well.

"The reincarnationists, those who believe in literal rebirth of an individual consciousness in the obstructed world, have obstructed the idea of quality and quantity. They have taken a partial truth and made it a hard-binding and destructive dogma."

She repeated some of what she had said before, presumably to be sure it related to the obstructed idea of reincarnation. "Destiny relates mainly to your plane: the destiny of purpose and quality. Freedom of choice to evolve happens in our unobstructed world. Here our freedom is unlimited. So why would anyone want to return to a limited part of life's adventure in the obstructed when free and limitless opportunities lie ahead? Here you can develop freely all aspects of your consciousness. Here, you can serve the great purpose of evolution. Here, you truly work out your karma.

"The reincarnationist answers, 'If I develop enough quantity in one lifetime, I can come back with a higher quality the next time.' But the universal law insists that evolution of quality takes place in the unobstructed world."

I asked, "Why is this so important? What harm does it do?"

Is Reincarnation an Illusion?

"The idea of reincarnation is a great glimpse. There is such a thing as reincarnation of quality of consciousness. Various degrees of quality of consciousness are constantly being reborn, but they should not be reborn as individual entities coming back. Individual consciousness does not die and should not be reborn in the obstructed. It should continue on my plane and on other planes beyond mine."

I wanted to know, "What happens when individuals come across?"

"Glad you asked," said Karen. "They bring with them quantity from their earth living. The individual keeps his personal quantity and a like amount goes into a general reservoir of quality of consciousness on this side. Earth parents, through their own spiritual quality and quantity, are then able to draw from the reservoir and pass on a specific quality to a newborn child.

"The child gradually acquires quantity and adds it to the reservoir of consciousness when she comes across. She leavens the spiritual level of the whole, much or little, depending on what she adds. Those who add little often wish they had lived more fully. This, in fact, is the equivalent of the final judgment. The judgment is one of self-condemnation for the lack of quantity contributed.

"And this is where the reincarnationist stumbles in. She judges herself, determines that she should have gained more quantity, and decides to try it again. Sadly, a second incarnation in the obstructed universe (and it does happen) scarcely adds to the pool of consciousness at all. The main purpose of consciousness—evolution—is not really advanced by literal reincarnation. The person who continues here and develops quality serves evolution better."

I was intrigued with the consistency of logic in Karen's description. But what about the many problems reincarnation theory seemed to solve? Certainly other mediums more talented than myself had promoted this theory. It did seem to answer the question of suffering, though it was beginning to look as if Karen's theory did too, and perhaps more intelligently. What about the often recognized feeling of deja vu, the feeling of having been there or experienced something before, that reincarnationists claim is explained by their theory. I let the pen run on at its own pace to see what came.

"Actually," said the writing, "reincarnation explains less than the idea of direct immortality. You note, Mom, that other psychics believed in reincarnation, but many do not. Often psychics of the reincarnation persuasion are accurate in making other predictions. They base much of their ability to predict or heal on the fact that they see past lives. Therefore, they claim to know why the person is now ill or behaving in a certain manner. However, they don't offer proof that the person actually did live such a life. They only claim it.

"Mediums who believe in direct immortality also heal, predict the future, and explain events by saying someone in the next world told them. And here, often more proof is more convincing. It is more impressive for Karen, or anyone here, to produce specific evidence of her own life that can be validated than to claim with no proof that she lived before.

"Mom, all any psychic can do is offer information for its inherent value and let others decide what to accept. I believe what I am telling you will be so logical that many will accept it."

I raised the same question I had earlier in this session. "What specific harm does this theory do?"

Karen answered directly this time. "Confusion creates serious difficulties for both worlds. When we come across, we are the same selves we've always been. We retain our personalities and prejudices. Those who come across believing in reincarnation still believe it over here. They attempt to reenter a body there and be reborn. This creates situations that the rest of us view with dismay.

"Your world is intended as a borning place where all life is new. Everyone is intended to be a first-time individual. If the reincarnationist is spiritually stronger than the new consciousness being born (and sometimes this is true, for they tend to select lower qualities to invade), he supplants that new consciousness. The new being, then, is not able to develop; on arrival here at death the being is only a partially developed consciousness. The two parts of the being usually separate here, and of course, this creates considerable confusion. Both need much help. And sadly, the reincarnationist may still be unconvinced and try again to be reborn.

"In other cases a person may choose to be reborn in a new consciousness of a higher quality. Then the newborn dominates and develops but still is considerably damaged by the interference. The reincarnated person is submerged and for a time becomes a lost soul. From this you can see our aversion to the concept of literal reincarnation.

"Reincarnation plays havoc with the development of quantity. And, by the way, we do not call this process reincarnation. We call it possession."

I was bothered. "If what you say is true, why do people try to reincarnate?"

"Those who firmly believe are difficult to convince. Such people believe they will be handicapped if they are not reborn. They assume that the only way to develop karma is to re-experience earth life.

"Also, many people are embedded in the physical. To us some of you look like those little plastic souvenir paperweights with tiny fish or plant life embedded in them; you are bits of frozen consciousness implanted in the material world. Once you postulate and accept that the unobstructed universe exists, once you believe that life is potentially more beautiful than anything on earth, you would think people would prefer it. Yet for many, the physical world is the real world. It's all they have, and they cling covetously to it. Poor souls!

"A psychological reason is more disturbing and difficult to combat. Some people reincarnate as a form of self-punishment because of guilt. The impact of coming across is devastating, for often they see vividly the mistakes they made. They experience a period of deep regret. Some desire so strongly to try again and do a better job (work out their karma) that they are difficult to convince that they will only compound their problems through such an effort.

"Worse, their guilt over past mistakes makes them want to punish themselves by repeating a miserable experience. 'If I can suffer this time for what I did before,'

Trying to reincarnate.

they say, 'then I can atone for the past.' We try to convince them that any atonement can be accomplished here, but this is futile if the guilt is very deep."

I wanted to know about individuals that claimed to be associated with the same people again and again over many lifetimes. "Why would they want this?"

Karen's answer showed a depressing aspect of human nature. "Attempted reincarnation is sometimes the result of a deep hostility toward others. Suppose that you and I were mother and daughter in the most recent life but might have been sisters in a previous life and a married couple at another time. They claim they can better correct the mistakes made with the same people. Could it not also be that they unconsciously desire to further punish another person for past injuries as well? A hostile individual would secretly desire this."

I asked another question. "Many claim that the common experience of deja vu is evidence of reincarnation. They say that the sense of having experienced a time or place before is simply the recognition of a previous life. Are they right?"

"Partially. You remember I told you that quantity of consciousness goes into a reservoir and is reborn. Although this is converted into quality, the memory of the quantity is left in the reservoir. This memory of life-experience can be reborn into a new consciousness, a new individual.

"This easily explains deja vu. Suppose a new individual acquires some of my quantity memory, perhaps the experience of being in the hospital in Los Angeles. At some point in his life, if he himself enters that hospital or one that looks like it, he will doubtless experience not only a strong feeling of having been there before but also some negative emotions connected with it.

"The fact that such experiences are fairly common among many people but are not consistently frequent in a given individual is more readily explained by the reincarnation of memory from the pool than by literal individual reincarnation.

"Have you ever considered the very curious circumstance that no one while on earth really

87

remembers a past experience of life. Do you? Did I? A few think they do. And granted, a very few parapsychologists cite cases of reincarnation in which very young children appear to remember past lives. These could just as well be cases of possession. They could also be cases of mediumship in which the child is telling the story of someone actually on my side but making it appear as if he is telling his own story. Thus no real proof of 'remembering' is given.

"Some say the memory of the past remains unconscious, but this is a cop-out. It would seem that if one is to correct past mistakes, work out his karma, he could do a better job of it if he remembered what went wrong before. Indeed, anything less would appear to be a kind of strange punishment of a most unethical universe.

"Endless repetition of experience that teaches nothing because nothing experienced is remembered, is the worst possible hell-a form of cruel and unusual punishment by a merciless God. At the very least, there is certainly an oddity in the confusion of going back to earth for fifty trips and learning so little."

I tuned in to Karen's last statements. The logic made sense. Karen's comments about the cruelty of trying to atone for past mistakes when one does not even remember them was a telling point. But I was still concerned about the concept of suffering, for I had always felt reincarnation was a logical explanation for seemingly inexplicable illness or poverty.

She was ready. "Can't you see how this is an oversimplified explanation for suffering?" she asked. "The reincarnationists have used their karma theory as a handy-dandy tool for explaining a very complex problem. The supreme level of consciousness is positive. No vindictive God metes out punishment with no opportunity to make amends nor any memory of past experience."

"But," I said, "your explanation that we bump up against laws we don't know about is equally disturbing. Why should I suffer for not knowing a law?"

"Because the universal law is put there for a larger purpose than causing or understanding suffering. It is in place to provide order and continuity for the entire *universe. We live in a universe of a complex system of moral and spiritual laws as well as physical ones. Inevitably, because of our limited earth-bound knowledge, we are going to make mistakes that will result in what we call suffering. However, knowledge of the law is accessible to us if we wish to investigate."*

That made sense.

I realized that Karen had effectively answered her own questions about why we are born and why we die. We are born as individual consciousnesses so that we can ultimately further the purpose of the evolution of all consciousness. We die for the same reason. Taking care to be born in the obstructed world only once gives an individual consciousness the greatest opportunity to serve the evolutionary purpose.

I will now quote one extract from "30 Years Among the Dead" where the mortal assumes the physical ailments of the attached spirit, to illustrate that attached spirits can indeed impress a variety of things into the mind of a mortal:

In the summer of 1923 a gentleman, Mr. I., consulted us about his wife, who for nine months had been confined to her bed suffering from intense pain in the head, diagnosed by others as due to brain tumor, and from a seemingly paralyzed condition of one arm, which was helpless.

We made several calls at the home of the invalid, giving electrical treatments which strengthened the patient, but Mrs. Wickland clairvoyantly saw the spirit of a man with a ghastly head wound and a woman with a crippled arm hovering about the lady.

At our next concentration circle, the spirit of this man controlled Mrs. Wickland, and we learned that in life he had been a house painter who had fallen from a scaffold, and, as he said, "split open" his head.

He did not know that he had died and declared that he was suffering from agonizing pains in the head, but that lately he had a very comfortable bed to rest in. Convinced of his true condition he was taken away, and from that time Mrs. I. had no further pain in the head.

She still remained in bed, however, feeling weak and suffering with the paralyzed arm. After another treatment we returned to our home, inviting Mr. I. to attend our concentration circle that evening.

When he came he said that after our departure his wife felt so much better that she had risen, and for the first time in nine months, spent the day out of bed.

The events of the evening, therefore, were of great interest to the gentleman, as the controlling spirit complained of pains corresponding exactly with those endured by his wife.

EXPERIENCE, JULY 17, 1923

**Spirit: MRS. Lizzy Davidson   Patient: MRS. I.
Psychic: MRS. WICKLAND**

The spirit held one arm pressed tightly to the body, moaning incessantly.

Doctor. Good evening. Have we some one here who it sick? Is this one who has passed out with some sickness, and still holds the trouble in his mind? What is the matter?
Spirit. (Groaning.) My arm! Oh, my arm!
Dr. What is the matter with it?
Sp. It hurts me.
Dr. What happened to it?
Sp. Where's my bed? I'm sick.
Dr. Are you sleepy?
Sp. I'm sick in bed. I ought to be in bed.
Dr. Haven't you been in bed long enough?
Sp. I'm awfully sick.
Dr. How many years have you been sick?
Sp. A long, long time.
Dr. How long is it since you died?
Sp. Died? I'm sick, I said. I am not dead. I said "sick." You do not know about me. I am so sick.
Dr. I realize that you are sick in your mind. Otherwise you are not sick.

Trying to reincarnate.

Sp.   Oh! Oh! I'm a very sick woman. Don't touch me! My arm! My arm!
Dr.   Was it hurt?
Sp.   Why did you take me away when I was so comfortable in bed? Oh, that nice, comfortable bed! (To Mr. I.) He (Dr. W.) took me away just when I was going to lie down and sleep.
Mr. I.   I am very glad to see you here.
Sp.   He took me along with him, and I wanted to sleep. I am a very sick woman.
Dr.   We are going to cure your arm.
Sp.   Oh, I want to be in that bed. It's so nice and comfortable. It's such a nice bed, and there is such a nice gentleman to wait on me.
Dr.   You will never be in that bed again.
Sp.   I am a very sick woman. You had better call a doctor.
Mr. G.   That gentleman is a doctor.
Dr.   How long have you been sick?
Sp.   (Recognizing Dr. W.) Why, you are the one who gave me those sparks! Take me away from him!
Mr. G.   That was an electrical treatment.
Sp.   He told me I should go with him. He said, "Any one who is around this lady, must come with me," so I went with him. Why did you tell me to come with you, and then hold me like this? (To Mr. I.) Can't you do something to protect me?
Mr. I.   This is a good place for you.
Sp.   You think so! Why did you let this man bring me here?
Mr. G.   He did not want you to make an invalid of his wife.
Sp.   Can't you tell this man to leave me alone? (To Mr. I)
Mr. I.   No, I think you are in good hands.
Sp.   No! No! No! I don't want to stay here! (Stamping feet furiously.)
Dr.   Do you want to hover around this gentleman's wife, and ruin her life?
Sp.   He can take care of us so nicely. I like him and I want to stay there! (Angrily stamping feet.)
Mr. I.   They will take good care of you here.

Is Reincarnation an Illusion?

Dr.   You are not sick, but you have a bad temper.
Sp.   I am sick with my arm.
Dr.   Only in your mind.
Sp.   Can't I go back to that bed? (To Mr. I.) You are such a nice nurse.
Dr.   You have been bothering his wife, hovering around her. That gentleman is taking care of his wife, and incidentally has been taking care of you. You are a spirit. He doesn't want you there any more.
Sp.   (Coaxingly to Mr. I.) Don't you want to take care of me again?
Mr. I.   No.
Sp.   You mean thing, you! (Crying)
Dr.   You must obtain understanding. Are you a cry baby?
Sp.   No, I am not a cry baby! (Stamping feet again.)
Dr.   Then it is just temper. Now behave, and understand that you have lost your mortal body.
Sp.   I have not lost my body.
Dr.   You have lost your physical body; that is in the grave.
Sp.   I am not in the grave!
Dr.   But your body is.
Sp.   My body is myself. No, I am not in the grave; this is my body.
Dr.   Look at your hands; they are not yours.
Sp.   Where did I get these rings? I had more stones in mine, didn't I? (To Mr. I.)
Mr. I.   My wife had.
Sp.   You gave me a nice ring.
Mr. I.   No, I did not. I gave it to my wife.
Sp.   Yes, you did.
Mr. I.   No, I did not.
Dr.   You are a selfish, Earthbound spirit.
Sp.   Spirit! I'm no spirit. I am a good woman, a good, religious woman. I love Jesus.
Dr.   Then why are you not with him? You have evidently been dead a long time.
Sp.   I say I am not dead! Oh! My arm, my arm.
Mr. G.   You forgot that you had a crippled arm. You have been moving it about.

Trying to reincarnate.

Sp. Yes, I forgot, but I know where my pains are! (Stamping feet.)
Dr. When you have a temper you forget your pains.
Sp. You do not! I have pains just the same. Don't you know that?
Dr. I know you have a temper.
Sp. I am a good Christian lady. I love Jesus with all my heart and all my soul. He is my Savior.
Mr. G. To save you from what?
Sp. From sin.
Dr. Then you cannot be so very good if you have sins.
Sp. Is that so? Say, are we in church? Look at all the people. Did you take me to church?
Dr. This is a place where we release Earthbound spirits.
Sp. Earthbound spirits? What are you talking about? Will you pray, and sing "Jesus, Lover of my Soul?"
Dr. No, we will not. Where did you come from?
Sp. I get so mad when I think of that bed. Why did you take me away from that nice bed? I feel so sad. My back and my arm hurt me so much. My arm is paralyzed. I was shot in my arm.
Dr. Who shot you?
Sp. Ask them.
Dr. Did they use a hypodermic?
Sp. Yes, that's what I mean. I would like to have one more shot. Will you give me just a little? Oh, please, just a little bit! Give me just a little shot in the arm.
Dr. Were you a drug addict?
Sp. I was sick such a long time, and I couldn't sleep, so they put something in my arm. They put it in so many times that my arm got sore, then it seemed to be paralyzed. They put in too much.
Dr. Well, now we must hurry; it is getting late.
Sp. What's the hurry? Where are you going - out?
Dr. We are going to help you understand your condition. You have lost your mortal body and, are a spirit. This is not your body.
Sp. Is that so? You only think so.

93

Is Reincarnation an Illusion?

Dr.   This is not your body at all; you are only borrowing it temporarily.
Sp.   How do you know?
Dr.   This is my wife's body.
Sp.   I never married you.
Dr.   I did not say that.
Sp.   You said I was your wife. Yes, you did! I heard it myself.
Dr.   I said you were talking through my wife's body.
Sp.   Have you ever heard of any one talking through another person's body?
Dr.   Tell us who you are.
Sp.   Hold my hand, not my arm.
Dr.   We will treat your arm, then it will be well. (Manipulating arm.)
Sp.   Oh! That electric man!
Dr.   Now your arm is not paralyzed at all. Look at your dress. Is it yours? Where did you get it?
Sp.   Did you buy this dress?
Dr.   My wife did. What is your name?
Sp.   Lizzie.
Dr.   Lizzie what?
Sp.   Mrs. Lizzie Davidson, and I don't want to be called Lizzie! When you speak to me, you must call me Mrs. Davidson.
Dr.   Now listen to me. I am telling you a fact when I say you have lost your own body, but you do not realize it. You have been bothering that gentleman's wife (Mrs. I.) for a long time. You have made her an invalid.
Sp.   I have not been his wife.
Dr.   No, but you have been bothering his wife.
Sp.   (Coquettishly, to Mr. I.) You are a nice nurse, and I like you. Don't you like me?
Mr. I.   No!
Sp.   I don't want your wife to go to sleep, because when she sleeps I can't stay, and I want to sleep in that nice bed, and have you wait on me.
Dr.   You have been keeping that lady awake all night.
Sp.   Because when she sleeps I have to go.
Dr.   That is selfishness.

Trying to reincarnate.

Sp.   I have no home, so I have to make my home with her. She's an awful nice lady.
Dr.   Now you will have to find a home of your own in the spirit world.
Sp.   Where is that?
Dr.   It is the invisible world about the Earth plane. Do you believe in Heaven?
Sp.   Yes, where God is, and Jesus Christ, and the Holy Ghost. I am going to Heaven.
Dr.   Use a little reason. You lost your physical body long ago.
Sp.   Where did I lose it?
Dr.   We cannot tell that.
Sp.   Then how did you find it out?
Dr.   You are proving the fact yourself. Do you realize that this is the hand of my wife that I am holding?
Sp.   You are holding my hand, and I am not your wife! (Stamping.)
Dr.   I am holding my wife's hands, and you are talking through her.
Sp.   You are not going to hold me any longer!
Dr.   You are talking to us, but we cannot see you. You are invisible to us. Every one here sees that this is my wife's body.
Mr. I.   Did you follow Dr. Wickland here this morning?
Sp.   He put those awful things in me. (Electricity.) Then he said: "Everybody come along with me!" (To. Dr. W.) Why did you do that and make me get out? And that Indian girl! (Silver Star, one of Mrs. Wickland's guides, who had controlled for a brief time that morning, telling funny stories to attract the spirit's attention.)
She made me laugh until I got so weak and sick that before I knew it I was away from that lady. I'm so mad! If I could only get hold of that Indian I would wring her neck all right!
Dr.   I thought you said you were a Christian?
Sp.   Yes, I am. God forgive me for saying that! Let me pray! I made a mistake.
Mr. I.   You said the doctor brought you here.
Sp.   He did not bring me in this body.

Is Reincarnation an Illusion?

Mr. I. That body has been here all day; you came with the doctor and his wife in their auto this morning.
Sp.   What do you mean by auto?
Dr.   Don't you know what an automobile is?
Sp.   What is it?
Dr.   It is a car that runs by itself. There are millions of them in use now. You lost your body evidently a long time ago.
Sp.   Are you sure about it? When did I lose it?
Dr.   I do not know. We do not know you.
Sp.   I told you I am Lizzie Davidson. Let us pray!
Dr.   I think you are two-faced.
Sp.   I think so, too, sometimes. Sometimes I have dark hair and sometimes light. (The patient had dark hair.)
Dr.   How can you explain that?
Sp.   I don't know, and I don't care. I only love Jesus.
Dr.   Where did you come from? Do you know where you are? You are in Los Angeles, California.
Sp.   I am not, I never have been, I never was. I had no money to go there.
Dr.   Where did you live?
Sp.   In New York.
Mr. I. Was it down on Twenty-seventh Street?
Sp.   No, it wasn't.
Dr.   It must be a long time since you were on Earth, for you have not seen automobiles that run without horses.
Sp.   Does the devil run them?
Dr.   No, internal combustion.
Sp.   Blab! Blab! Internal combustion.
Dr.   What year do you think this is? We think it is 1923.
Sp.   Then you're off. It is 1883.
Dr.   Who is President?
Sp   Don't you know?
Mr. G. Yes, we know, but we want to see if you know.
Dr.   I think it is Harding.
Sp.   Wait a little; I have to think. It is Arthur. Garfield was shot in 1881, in July.
Dr.   Is that the last you remember? Can you recall any President later than that?

Trying to reincarnate.

Sp. No, just Arthur. He became President after Garfield was shot.
Dr. We have had many Presidents since then: Cleveland, Harrison, Taft and many others.
Sp. I had a brother-in-law named Cleveland.
Dr. Was he the President?
Sp. Not much! He didn't know very much anyway. What kind of people are you?
Dr. We are all investigators. Do you know what becomes of the dead?
Sp. They go to Heaven, and see Christ and the Holy Ghost and the Father, sitting on the throne, and the people sitting at His feet. I love Jesus! I never loved anybody as much as I do Jesus!
Dr. You say it is 1883; that is forty years ago. It is 1923 now. Why are you not in "Heaven" since you have been dead all that time?
Sp. I have not been dead.
Dr. You are dead only to the world; you lost your physical body forty years ago.
Sp. How do you know?
Dr. From your own words. We are now listening to what people call a dead person. You are talking through my wife's body.
Sp. (Seeing a spirit.) Who is that over there?
Dr. Ask them who they are.
Sp. There's Cleveland, my brother-in-law. Hell! What do you want?
Mr. G. Hello, Cleveland! How are you today?
Sp. (Angrily, to Mr. G.) You keep still! You don't know him.
Mr. G. What was his business?
Sp. He was a shoemaker.
Mr. G. He was probably a good one.
Sp. He was not nice to my sister. I don't like you, Cleveland! You always made trouble.
Dr. Listen to what he says.
Sp. (To spirit, Cleveland.) You devil, you!
Dr. That is fine talk for a Christian.
Sp. God forgive me! God forgive me!
Dr. Be serious and forgive Cleveland.

97

Sp.	I will never forgive him - never! He went away and took my sister with him. (To spirit.) You devil! You went away with my sister and it broke my heart when you took her. Not now, nor in the world to come, will I ever forgive you - no, not much! Get away there!
Dr.	Is that Christian charity? Is that the teaching of Christ?
Sp.	People forget themselves sometimes.
Dr.	You will have to forgive him, and ask him to forgive you.
Sp.	I will ask forgiveness from Christ. From Cleveland I never will.
Dr.	Jesus said: "Forgive, and ye shall be forgiven."
Sp.	Yes, but nobody practices it. I will pray and that will help.
Dr.	No, it will not. Praying won't help you any in this case. You have been in darkness forty years.
Sp.	Sometimes I have been a man, and sometimes a lady.
Dr.	You have been obsessing people.
Sp.	Here, you Cleveland, you have no business to come here and torment me again. What have you done with my sister, you devil, you?
Dr.	I thought you belonged to the Holy of Holies.
Sp.	Cora! (Spirit.) My sister! Why did you go with that man? I will never forgive him. I suffered so much. I thought you would be with me for the rest of your life. I promised mother I would take care of you all my life then you ran away with that thing! You broke my heart.
Dr.	What does she say?
Sp.	No - she says she loved him. There is no such thing as loving any man. Say, there's David, too! I suppose you think you are going to make up with me. Not much you aren't! I never will forgive you either.
Dr.	Who is David?
Sp.	My husband.
Dr.	What was the matter with him?
Sp.	He was a fool.

Trying to reincarnate.

Dr.   For marrying you?
Sp.   The world is coming to an end! People are so full of sin that God does not know what to do with them. He will have to teach them in some way, so let us pray! I want to go to Heaven.
Dr.   Do you think you have much chance of getting there?
Sp.   I will pray for you. You know, David, you were no good. I have had my troubles.
Dr.   Didn't you have any faults?
Sp.   No, I prayed to God.
Dr.   Doesn't your conscience bother you?
Sp.   My conscience?
Dr.   Yes. Doesn't it make you feel guilty?
Sp.   Cora, you always loved me, and you said you would always be with me for the rest of your life, and then you ran away with that thing.
Dr.   What does she say?
Sp.   Cora says: "You did not let me go anywhere. It was always church, church, and you wanted me to pray all the time. I got tired of it, and then Cleveland came, and he promised to give me a home. He was very good to me." But I will not forgive him anyhow.
Dr.   You were a religious fanatic, and your sister could not stand it.
Sp.   She ought to love Jesus.
Dr.   You have not found Jesus yourself.
Sp.   I haven't found Jesus because I am not dead.
Dr.   Will you not believe what your sister says to you? Where did she live?
Sp.   She lived in New York, then moved to Chicago.
Dr.   Ask her whether she is a spirit.
Sp.   She says she's dead. (To sister.) You're dead, and you deserve it, too, because you became a spiritualist at the last, you crazy thing, you! I got mad at you because you ran around to spiritualist meetings all the time. That Cleveland took you because he belonged there and believed in spirits!
Dr.   I am sitting here with my wife, and you, an invisible spirit, are talking to us through her.

99

Is Reincarnation an Illusion?

Dr.   Does your sister say anything further?
Sp.   She says: "Lizzie, come to your senses!" You don't need to tell me that! Shut up with you! They have crushed me.
Dr.   Were you always selfish?
Sp.   No. David, he was a good man at times. He always worked and took care of me. I had a good home, but he did not want me to go to church so much. He wouldn't pay his money to the church, so I got mad and called him a stingy fool. I told him if he did not go to church, and pay money to the Lord, he would go to hell. And there he is!
Dr.   He is not in hell.
Sp.   Yes, he is - but I don't see how he skipped out. David, you died a long time ago and I have prayed for you because I thought you were in hell, and you should have stayed there, because you did not pay any money to the Lord.
Dr.   Ask him if he has been in hell.
Sp.   He says: "No, there is no such place." You big fool, you are in hell!
Dr.   You yourself are in the hell of ignorance. You are bound by selfishness and ignorance.
Sp.   Now, David, don't you bother me. You go to hell, because you belong there. You did not go to church.
Dr.   Jesus said: "Judge not that ye be not judged!"
Sp.   I have been born again in the blood of Jesus. I paid all the money I could to the church.
Dr.   And kept yourself in ignorance.
Sp.   I have been baptized, immersed, and I am one of the holiest. I was a good church member. I worked hard for my money and have suffered, so I will go to Heaven when I die.
Dr.   You never will really die.
Sp.   David is dead.
Dr.   If he himself were "dead" he could not talk to you.
Sp.   Cora died in Chicago.
Dr.   If they are "dead" how can they talk to you?
Sp.   (Frightened.) Why - they are ghosts! I forgot they are dead.

Trying to reincarnate.

Dr.   Ghosts like yourself. You are a ghost.
Sp.   But they are dead.
Dr.   Do they look as if they were dead?
Sp.   No, they look much prettier than they did before. I suppose they are in Heaven. (To the spirits.) Have you folks seen Christ and God? Have you been in Heaven with Them?
Dr.   What do they say?
Sp.   They say: "No!" Then you are - I thought so - then you have been in hell. Have you? They say: "No!"
Dr.   Ask them if the body you are using is yours.
Sp.   (To invisibles.) Well, what are you looking at? Don't you know me? They say, not as I look now. How is that?
Dr.   Have I not been telling you that you are invisible to us, and that you are using my wife's body?
Sp.   How?
Dr.   Spirits can control mortals as you are now doing. Jesus cast out unclean spirits.
Sp.   Unclean! I'm not unclean. You insult me again.
Dr.   You influenced that gentleman's wife, disturbed her life and made an invalid of her.
Mr. I.   Don't you recognize me?
Sp.   Yes, you are a very good nurse, and I think I should like to have you nurse me again.
Dr.   He was not nursing you, he was nursing his wife.
Sp.   We had such a nice bed; I just love it. You tell your wife that she must not get up, because if she does I can't stay.
Dr.   You will never go there again.
Mr. I.   My wife is up now. She has been up the whole day.
Sp.   I want her in bed.
Mr. I.   She has been up since the doctor left this morning. She had to remain in bed for nine months.
That Indian girl made me laugh so hard that I could not stay with that nice lady. It makes me so mad! I was listening to what the Indian said, and I laughed so hard at her that I lost control of the lady. (To Mr. I.) What did you come here for?
Dr.   He wanted to get rid of you.
Mr. I.   I came here to see you tonight.

Is Reincarnation an Illusion?

Sp.   (Coyly.) Were you lonesome for me?

Mr. I.   (Emphatically.) No!

Sp.   I would like to go back with you, can I?

Mr. I.   No, you cannot.

Dr.   You were very selfish, but you will not acknowledge it.

Sp.   Here's my sister Cora and her husband, Cleveland, and my husband, David. No, no! Oh, there's my mother! Did you come from Heaven, Mother? Are you happy in Heaven, Mother, with Jesus and God?

Dr.   What does she say?

Sp.   She says: "Lizzie, behave yourself." Now, Mother, I was always a good girl to you. Mother says: "You were always selfish, Lizzie."

Dr.   That comes from your own mother. Your conscience tells you the same thing. You had a mean disposition - ask your mother.

Sp.   Mother, did you come from Heaven? Mother, I'm not dead yet, so I can't go to Heaven. I have to die before I can go there.

Dr.   The Bible says: "Ye are the temple of God and the Spirit of God dwelleth in you." Where will you find that God outside of yourself?

Sp.   It says in the Bible that God sits on a throne, with Christ on His right hand.

Dr.   The Bible says: "God is Love and he that dwelleth in Love dwelleth in God." Where will you find such a God?

Sp.   In Heaven.

Dr.   Jesus said: "God is Spirit, and they that worship Him must worship Him in Spirit and in truth." Did you do that? No, you simply accepted a dogma, and pretended you were saintly but your conscience condemned you all the time, did it not?

Sp.   I was not happy.

Dr.   Your conscience tells you that you were a hypocrite.

Sp.   How do you know it does?

Dr.   Your actions show that. Does your mother say anything more?

Trying to reincarnate.

Sp. She says: "Lizzie, behave yourself." What does she say that for? She was always after me, because she says I had such a tongue.

Dr. You must change your attitude, or the spirit forces will take you away and place you in a dark dungeon.

Sp. God forgive me! I will pray.

Dr. You are not sincere.

Sp. (To Mr. I.) Will you forgive me?

Dr. If you are sincere in asking, he will.

Sp. David, you were always good to me, but I was not always a good wife to you. I thought you were a devil, and I always talked about you - yes, I did. (Crying.)

Dr. Crying will not help you.

Sp. David, I loved you anyhow. Do you like me, David? I was your dear little wife. He says, "Shame on you!" and that I was nice when I did not have a temper.

Dr. Now you must hurry and go.

Sp. I want to ask that nice man to please forgive me. (To Mr. I.) Will you?

Mr. I. Yes.

Sp. Cleveland, I was mad at you. You were good to my sister, but why did you go away? Why did you go to Chicago and take her away from me? He says his business was there.
(To Mr. I.) Will you forgive me? I mean it, I really mean it this time - will you? If I never meant it in my life before, I do now. Mother, will you forgive me? Will you? I love you. I was very selfish; I know now. I can see it now; I see everything now. My eyes have been opened. Oh, oh! (Crying.)

Dr. Crying does no good. Listen to what your relatives say.

Sp. Can I go with them to Heaven?

Dr. Forget "Heaven," and be sensible. You will never find God as you have imagined. You must be honest with yourself.

Is Reincarnation an Illusion?

Sp.	I have never, in all my life, been so humiliated as I have been tonight. You forgive me, David, don't you? And you, Cora, and Cleveland, too?
Dr.	Do you know that you are in California?
Sp.	How did I get there?
Dr.	You evidently have been "dead" some forty years. No one actually dies, but the physical body is lost, and people call that "death."
Sp.	Part of the time I have been walking, but for a very long time I have had such a good time in that nice bed.
Dr.	Yes, disturbing that gentleman's wife.
Sp.	But he has been so good to me; he's so nice.
Dr.	Aren't you ashamed to make an invalid of a poor mortal?
Sp.	David, will you take me along with you?
Dr.	Now you must go.
Sp.	I am going. (Rising.)
Dr.	You cannot go that way.
Sp.	How in the world will I go then? That Indian girl won't take me away, will she?
Dr.	She will teach you beautiful truths.
Sp.	But she laughed at me.
Dr.	Now think yourself with your relatives and you will be there.
Sp.	Now I will go. Will I see God?
Dr.	Forget that. You do not have the right understanding of God.
Sp.	Goodbye!
	After this Mrs. I. recovered her strength and was soon walking and driving about.[72]

Included in the book, "30 Years among the Dead" is a discussion with the lady who started this movement, Madam Blavatsky herself. Rather than quoting the extensive message, I will simply quote her apparently altered views on reincarnation:

EXPERIENCE, NOVEMBER 1, 1922

---

[72] *30 Years among the dead*, Chapter 9, pages 193-203

Trying to reincarnate.

Spirit: MADAM BLAVATSKY   Psychic: MRS. WICKLAND

I wanted to come to you this evening. I believe in the work this little circle is doing, and I am very pleased with the work you are carrying on. I wish there were more to help us, to meet us on a half way basis to understand there is no death.

....

To me came Reincarnation. It appealed to me for a time. I could not see the truth clearly. I felt that it was very unjust some should be rich and have such good times and that others should be poor and have so much trouble. Others did not get enough Earth experience-at least so I felt.

I studied Reincarnation, and I thought there was truth and justice in the theory that we come back and learn and have more experiences. I taught it and wanted to bring it out to the world and its peoples.

I felt that I remembered far back in my past. I felt I knew all about my past, but I was mistaken.

Memories of "past lives" are caused by spirits that bring such thoughts and represent the lives they lived. A spirit impresses you with the experiences of its life and these are implanted in your mind as your own. You then think you remember your past.

When you study, especially when you study Theosophy, you develop your mind and live in an atmosphere of mind. You remove yourself as much as possible from the physical. Naturally you become sensitive, and naturally you feel the spirits around you.

They speak to you by impressions and their past will be like a panorama. You feel it, and you live over the past of spirits and you make the mistake of taking this for the memory of former incarnations.

Is Reincarnation an Illusion?

> *I did not know this when I lived. I took it for granted that these memories were true, but when I came to the spirit side of life I learned differently.* [73]

In this chapter we have explored some incidents where a spirit has tried to reincarnate, and ended up attached to the mortal. In this condition, memories of the spirit were accessible by the mortal. We have also looked at some related incidents where physical ailments initially experienced by the spirit while alive, now become expressed by the mortal, when that spirit attaches itself to the mortal. Finally, Madam Blavatsky, as a spirit herself, explains that the source of past life memories is the real memories of adjacent spirits, and that these are "impressed" onto the mind of the mortal.

In this chapter we have considered that a possible source of past life memories is the real memories of adjacent or attached spirits. Whether that is the most common source is not known, as advanced spirits have commented that sometimes they have no idea where the memories come from. It also seems likely that memories that people recall while under hypnosis, or spontaneously may be from a more central memory bank, such as the Akashic Record.

---

[73] *30 Years among the Dead*, Chapter 15, page 351

Chapter 8

The soul and the spirit body.

We come now to the topic that completely demolished my existing belief system when I first read it. I realize that there are a few different conceptions of what we consist of, but the simplest and most sensible that I have ever found is that given by James Padgett. He channeled that we consist of three parts, a mortal body, a spirit body, and a soul. The spirit body could also be called an astral body, although it seems to have probably an astral body as well as another more etheric body used in higher planes. This may be a simplification, but it is a concept that makes a lot of sense. The soul is the real "you," and as you grow spiritually, you grow your soul. The spirit body reflects that soul, and the more advanced you are, the more light you will emit, and the more advanced and beautiful will that spirit appear. The soul itself is said to be pure spirit, and non-material, whereas the spirit body is semi-material.

Now he did not channel anything about the Indwelling Spirit mentioned in an earlier chapter, but as the Indwelling Spirit is not actually "us," I don't consider that a significant flaw in the description. When we astral travel, the spirit body travels, enclosing the soul, and is linked back to the mortal body by the well known silver chord. The mind seems to be a part of the spirit body, because it certainly travels. However, with recent advances in quantum mechanics, and in particular concepts like remote entanglement, I am beginning to wonder if this "travel" is another illusion. But it certainly seems to be travel.

The essence of this communication is that a soul, a pristine original soul, does not have a spirit body, and as a result, neither spirits nor mortals can see souls until after they incarnate. But once a soul incarnates, it gains a spirit body, and never again loses that spirit body. Probably the very act of incarnation causes this spirit body to be created. But, a soul encased in a spirit body, cannot be born into an embryo. It can only attach, as in the examples we saw from Dr. Irene Hickman and Dr. Carl Wickland.

Is Reincarnation an Illusion?

This makes great sense, because we do know that "we" are protected, and we don't get "deposed" by the next spirit that fancies a home in our body. Something prevents this, because as we can see, some spirits certainly do try to invade our space. In fact, this particular point is covered in "Astral Travel," in a rather unsavoury tale that I am somewhat loathe to cover, and I would like to make it quite clear that I do not under any circumstances support the procedure reported here, and that the following process is, in my opinion, certain to attract "bad Karma," or error, or sin or whatever you wish to call it. In other words, don't do this!

> With your present knowledge you can travel out and possess another body for any length of time you wish. Suppose there is someone whom you wish to influence, or whom you wish to become acquainted with. Travel astrally to where he is asleep and watch him. You will see his astral self depart from the body on its own affairs. He has in effect left his body double-parked and idling as he might leave his car double-parked and idling as he pops into a shop to get some cigarettes. This is your chance. Slip into that idling body and run it around for a little while. How does it feel to be that most dread of all spirits, a "possessing entity?"
>
> Not only can you run his body around – drive his car – but now you can avail yourself of a matchless opportunity to learn how he thinks and what makes him tick. When you have learned what you need to know through being in his body, lay the body carefully down again – park the borrowed car without damaging it – and go and get into your own car.[74]

I suspect that tale will upset you as much as it upset me. Folks that think you can joyride other cars, probably do think it's no worse joyriding a human body. I can't think of a more severe invasion of privacy, and contravention of free will. Because nobody would ever be happy at the thought that their "idling" body is being run around the block by someone who just fancies getting a feel of them. I have no

---

[74] *Astral Travel*, page 193.

The soul and the spirit body.

doubt that were they to ask the higher consciousness for permission, as does Irene Hickman, they would never be joyriding any bodies.

But, aside from the dreadful morality of this practice, it illustrates how much control can be exercised by an attached spirit, or even perhaps just an adjacent spirit. Obviously it is pretty much full control. It also illustrates that even while we are "alive" – incarnate – we can do pretty much everything that a discarnate entity can do.

To get back to the explanation that was given as to why spirits cannot reincarnate, this was channeled by a Dr Samuels, in 1955:[75]

> *I am here again to write you about a subject that has created interest among you, the Doctor and others, and that is the article on reincarnation. In the Padgett messages, various communications dealt with the falsity and absurdity of this Oriental doctrine, which holds that the human soul can reincarnate from one fleshly body to others in succession over periods of time and that as a result the soul has an opportunity to lessen its desire to sin and thus finally achieve purification while in the flesh.*
> *If you will examine the question a little more closely, you will see the impossibility of the soul in the spirit world to be reincarnated in the flesh for the reason that the soul, for this supposed phenomenon, would have to shed the spirit body in order to enter into a mortal body, since the soul is incased in a spirit body which is physical in nature but not of a gross material of what mortals call the material world, and that spirit body, which is the envelope and protector of the soul, is that which gives the soul its individuality as a conscious entity and remains with the soul so long as the soul lives. In the spirit world no spirit body has ever been deprived of its soul, and no spirit body thus hypothetically divested of its soul has ever died or been disintegrated, or has disappeared from its habitat, except as it advances from one sphere to another while making progress either to the sixth sphere or spiritual paradise or to the Celestial Heavens and Immortality.*

---

[75] Reincarnation is an oriental doctrine – https://new-birth.net/link9/ received March 10th 1955.

Is Reincarnation an Illusion?

As far as is known today by us in the spirit world, the spirit, that is to say, the soul and its spirit body, may live for all Eternity, if God so requires it, even if it does not possess the consciousness of immortality through possession of Divine Love, and it will certainly continue to live throughout all Eternity - the soul and its indissoluble spirit body - if it does possess the Divine Love, Immortality and At-onement with the Father.

As soul cannot be taken from, or torn from - or in any other way deprived of - its spirit body, once it has come to the spirit world, it would be equally impossible for the spirit body to enter the human body of another human being, for only a soul without a spirit body can enter a human body, and on the death of this body, the soul manifests its spirit body. The doctrine of reincarnation is, therefore utterly without foundation, for it is impossible, let me repeat, for a soul with its spirit body to enter a human body to be born again in the flesh.

When a human being dies in the flesh, his soul has already achieved under ordinary circumstances the purpose of his creation, that is, individualization and the creation of receptacles for soul's, and in his spirit body, in size, shape, appearance and nature, is the complete creation without the envelope of flesh.

This soul appears in the spirit world laden with the inharmonies of its Earth life, but since it has the opportunity of eliminating these inharmonies and becoming a purified soul in the spirit world through the exercise of its will and moral force and repentance, or becoming a Divine Angel through prayer to the Father for His Divine Love and Mercy, transforming the soul into the very essence of the Father, it is therefore absolutely unnecessary for the soul to go back to the flesh for another chance to purify itself, for the loving and merciful Heavenly Father had already provided a plan that would enable the soul - the real man - to attain purification, and here God showed Himself to be more merciful than He might have been had He decreed successive trials in the flesh for the process of purification, for man while thus seeking to purify his soul, would at the same time have to contend with the sinful influence of the flesh, and his

The soul and the spirit body.

> *ultimate purification would thus indefinitely be delayed or perhaps never accomplished until the very end of time. You can thus see that God has shown His Love for His created children by providing a way for them to be purged of their sins, while being free of baleful influences of the flesh, which would only hinder, and make more difficult, their tortuous progress toward purification.*

I guess if this explanation resonates with you, I need find no other explanations. Although I personally found this a "flawless" explanation, I do know that sadly some folks were not impressed by it. I guess it has everything to do with whether you accept that we consist of three parts, and that once we lose the mortal body, it is not possible to shed that spirit body. Because if you feel we can somehow shed the spirit body, then clearly we could incarnate as if we were a pristine un-incarnated soul. But of course shedding that spirit body is pretty much destroying who that spirit now is. And this is the point, as our mind is so wrapped up in the spirit body, and external to the physical. If one were to destroy the spirit body, it would be destroying all that that entity is.

However, on the face of it, it is plausible, because we do know that psychics can see spirits, and what they see is the spirit body. If advanced spirits tell us they cannot see souls, unless and until they have incarnated, then one is inclined to believe that. The final key in the puzzle is accepting that spirits never "throw off" their spirit body, and I guess one has to take that as a given, because from our mortal perch we are never going to be able to prove that.

Chapter 9

Sleeping Survivors.

We come now to an intriguing topic. The very first time I read about this, in the The Urantia Book, I simply dismissed it out of hand. Frankly a few things in The Urantia Book do not seem to accord with what those of us who deal with spirit believe we know. I have since learned that sadly the individual who was behind the book, one Dr. William Sadler, was so very against "spiritualism" that in a few places his personal opinions have probably been recorded in that book. When you read things like:

> Those who go to the mansion worlds are not permitted to send messages back to their loved ones. It is the policy throughout the universes to forbid such communication during the period of a current dispensation.[76]

And

> But it should be made clear that the midway creatures are not involved in the sordid performances taking place under the general designation of "spiritualism." The midwayers at present on Urantia, all of whom are of honorable standing, are not connected with the phenomenon of so-called 'mediumship'; and they do not, ordinarily, permit humans to witness their sometimes necessary physical activities or other contacts with the material world, as they are perceived by human senses.[77]

Well you could have blown me over when I read that. What absolute rubbish! I have a good friend, George Barnard, who has been dealing with these same midwayers for nigh on 60 years. He has written five

---

[76] *The Urantia Book*, Paper 112, Part 3, page 1230.
[77] *The Urantia Book*, Paper 77, Part 8, page 865.

books of his experiences, and published three so far.[78] If you are one of the estimated ten million people seeing the 11:11 time signal today, it is these very same midwayers who are in action. I consider them my brothers and sisters, and wish I could see them, in the way that George can. As far as I am aware, they are helping untold numbers of Light Workers around the globe, and they certainly get involved in mediumship.

I might diverge into an interesting by-product. If I find things that are wrong in the The Urantia Book, why do I consider that the book is worthwhile? Surely to be useful, a book must be 100% truth? This may well be the way we expect our spiritual sources to be, but I do not think there is any source that is 100% reliable. If God Himself wrote a book, and actually caused it to materialize, and nobody was required to "edit" it, or otherwise add to it, before you were able to buy it in a store, you would have just such a perfect source. But God has not done that, not even for the Bible. Now of course God could do such a thing, so the question is: "Why has he not?" The only answer I can come up with is that the ability to discern Truth is extremely valuable, and it is one of the things we have to learn while here. Confusion is almost certainly intended.

So how do we discern Truth? Well this is where you get the intellectuals throwing around things like Occam's Razor, and other tools of intellectual or scientific research. But spiritual truth is not like scientific truth. We have developed intellectual tools for advancing science, and these serve us well.

Nevertheless, scientists know that the entire theory of something can be discredited by a new finding, and they have to dismantle an entire "house" of cards, and start again with this new foundation, to arrive at a new "house" of cards. Folks tend to forget that all science is but a house of cards. Because the basis of scientific theory is that something be repeatable, folks sometimes attribute too much veracity to that theory. Sure it is our current best view of the world, and it's repeatable but it may be wrong.

---

[78] *The Search for 11:11*, by George Mathieu Barnard published by 11:11 Publishers, ISBN 1-931254-11-7 and *In the Service of 11:11*, by George Mathieu Barnard, published by 11:11 Publishers, ISBN 0-9577889-5-9 and *the anatomy of the halfway realm* published by 11:11 Publishers ISBN:0-9577889-7-8

Sleeping Survivors.

But spiritual truth is different. You really don't want to be in the situation of basing all your beliefs on a foundation that can be shown to be false. Doubtless that is why most religious organizations like to attribute some special value to their holy book. Study the Muslims, and you will see that they defend their holy book, the Koran, just as assiduously as do Christians the Bible. Maintaining that your faith is true, because it is based on an infallible holy book is a good simple marketing strategy, certainly if you want billions of followers. But of course, it really has no basis other than a hope that book truly is the unadulterated word of God. It is quite obvious that God knew we would have this problem with defining spiritual truth. And fortunately for us, He provided a way to discern spiritual Truth.

We do not need to build a logical framework in order to discern a spiritual truth. Of course, building logical frameworks is the way our minds work, so that can't easily be turned off, and in fact it is that very logical framework that often works against our discernment of new Truths. Sadly, if something does not fit an existing framework, we don't like to consider it. And if it shakes our framework, we often just ignore it.

Long before I discovered **why** I could discern Truth, I had already discovered that some sources of information had an ability to resonate with my soul. This is surely true of parts of the Bible, but I discovered this intriguing situation when I first came across the Padgett Messages. I guess I was at that time really focused on knowing truth, and up to that point I had read a lot that while feasible, did not "resonate." I also discovered this phenomenon while reading The Urantia Book. I am sure I could have this phenomenon manifest itself anywhere that I need to discern a spiritual Truth. Equally, I have found untruth reveal itself. What is this mechanism? Well it is called the Spirit of Truth, and it is in every sense a spirit such as the Holy Spirit, which many people will tell you they have experienced in their lives. I could tell you about that too, but that is another story.

How do you feel the Spirit of Truth? In my case I really do feel something inside me. I then have to concentrate on whether this is telling me that the passage is true or false. It does happen that I can tell that my soul, because that is where I believe I feel the sensation, likes the passage, but my mind does not. This has happened a few times to me, particularly reading The Urantia Book. Perhaps if I had read fewer

Is Reincarnation an Illusion?

spiritual books before I read that book, I might not have noticed this to quite the degree that I did. It is very unsettling when your mind disagrees with your soul. I have had to develop a technique to allow me to survive these intellectual stresses. I have a mental in-box, and when I find something like that, it goes there, sometimes for months on end. If my mind is unhappy, it may mean I have to unwind quite a few concepts, before I can adjust and accept this new truth. And, in many cases I am unwilling to simply do that, in the absence of any exterior validation. Sleeping survivors was just such a topic, although initially it did not even make the in-box, I thought it too preposterous. But fortunately I did not entirely forget about it.

What are sleeping survivors? Apparently some mortals, after death, do not awake, and may sleep even up to 1000 years or longer. They are awakened all together, at the end of a "dispensation." Well it would not surprise me if you too have never heard such a thing, and we surely have plenty of psychics around, talking to spirit. Let me quote here what The Urantia Book says:

> *From time to time, on motion of the planetary authorities or the system rulers, special resurrections of the sleeping survivors are conducted. Such resurrections occur at least every millennium of planetary time, when not all but "many of those who sleep in the dust awake." These special resurrections are the occasion for mobilizing special groups of ascenders for specific service in the local universe plan of mortal ascension. There are both practical reasons and sentimental associations connected with these special resurrections.*[79]

Later on, I read "Letters from a living dead man" and there I found a whole letter from David Hatch, relating how he had found many individuals fast asleep. In fact in such a deep sleep that they could not be roused. He then discusses this with his teacher, and the latter agrees to wake one example.

> *Many times during the months in which I have been here have I seen men and women lying in a state of unconsciousness more profound than the deepest sleep,*

---

[79] *The Urantia Book*, Paper 49, Part 6, page 568.

Sleeping Survivors.

their faces expressionless and uninteresting. At first, before I understood the nature of their sleep, I tried as an experiment to awaken one or two of them, and was not successful.

In certain cases where my curiosity was aroused, I have returned later, day after day, and found them still lying in the same lethargy.

"Why," I asked myself, "should any man sleep like that- a sleep so deep that neither the spoken word nor the physical touch could arouse him?"

One day when the Teacher was with me we passed one of those unconscious men whom I had seen before, had watched, and had striven unsuccessfully to arouse.

"Who are these people who sleep like that?" I asked the Teacher; and he replied:

"They are those who in their Earth life denied the immortality of the soul after death."

"How terrible!" I said. "And will they never awaken?"

"Yes, perhaps centuries, perhaps ages hence, when the irresistible law of rhythm shall draw them out of their sleep into incarnation. For the law of rebirth is one with the law of rhythm."

"Would it not be possible to awaken one of them, this man, for instance?"

"You have attempted it, have you not?" the Teacher inquired, with a keen look into my face.

"Yes," I admitted.

"And you failed?"

"Yes."

We looked at each other for a moment, then I said:

"Perhaps you, with your greater power and knowledge, could succeed where I have failed."

He made no answer. His silence fired my interest still farther, and I said eagerly:

"Will you not try? Will you not awaken this man?"

"You know not what you ask," he replied.

"But tell me this," I demanded: "could you awaken him?"

"Perhaps. But in order to counteract the law which holds him in sleep, the law of the spell he laid upon his own soul when he went out of life demanding unconsciousness and annihilation - in order to counteract that law, I should have to put in operation a law still stronger."

"And that is?" I asked.

"Will," he answered, "the potency of will."

"Could you?"

"As I said before - perhaps."

"And will you?"

"Again I say that you know not what you ask."

"Will you please explain?" I persisted, "for indeed this seems to me to be one of the most marvelous things which I have seen."

The face of the Teacher was very grave, as he answered:

"What good has this man done in the past that I should place myself between him and the law of cause and effect which he has willfully set in operation?"

"I do not know his past," I said.

"Then," the Teacher demanded, "will you tell me your reason for asking me to do this thing?"

"My reason?"

"Yes. Is it pity for this man's unfortunate condition, or is it scientific curiosity on your own part?"

I should gladly been able to say that it was pity for the man's sad state which moved me so; but one does not juggle with truth or with motives when speaking to such a Teacher, so I admitted that it was scientific curiosity.

"In that case," he said, "I am justified in using him as a demonstration of the power of the trained will."

"It will not harm him, will it?"

"On the contrary. And though he may suffer shock, it will probably be the means of so impressing his mind that never again, even in future lives on Earth, can he believe himself, or teach others to believe, that death ends everything. As far as he is concerned, he does not deserve that I should waste upon him so great an amount of energy as will be necessary to arouse him from this sleep, this spell which he laid upon himself ages ago. But if I awaken him, it will be for your sake, 'that you may believe.'"

Sleeping Survivors.

I wish I could describe the scene which took place, so that you could see it with the eyes of your imagination. There lay the man at our feet, his face colourless and expressionless, and above him towered the splendid form of the Teacher, his face beautiful with power, and his eyes brilliant with thought.

"Can you not see," asked the Teacher, "a faint light surrounding this seemingly lifeless figure?"

"Yes, but the light is very faint indeed."

"Nevertheless," said the Teacher, "that light is far less faint than is this weak soul's hold upon the eternal truth. But where you see only a pale light around the recumbent form, I see in that light many pictures of the soul's past. I see that he not only denied the immortality of the soul's consciousness, but that he taught his doctrine of death to other men and made them even as himself. Truly he does not deserve that I should try to awaken him!"

"Yet you will do it?"

"Yes, I will do it."

I regret that I am not permitted to tell you by what form of words and by what acts my Teacher succeeded, after a mighty effort, in arousing that man from his self-imposed imitation of annihilation. I realised as never before - not only the personal power of the Teacher, but the irresistible power of a trained and directed will.

I thought of that scene recorded in the New Testament, where Jesus said to the dead man in the tomb, "Lazarus, come forth!"

"The soul of man is immortal," declared the Teacher, looking fixedly into the shrinking eyes of the awakened man and holding them by his will.

"The soul of man is immortal," he repeated. Then in a tone of command: "Stand up!"

The man struggled to his feet. Though his body was light as a feather, as are all our bodies here, I could see that his slumbering energy was still almost too dormant to permit of that really slight exertion.

"You live," declared the Teacher. "You have passed through death, and you live. Do not dare to deny that you live. You cannot deny it."

119

Is Reincarnation an Illusion?

"But I do not believe -" began the man, his stubborn materialism still challenging the truth of his own existence, his memory surviving the ordeal through which he had passed. This last surprised me more than anything else. But after a moment's stupefaction I understood that it was the power of the Teacher's mental picture of the astral records round this soul, which had forced those memories to awaken.

"Sit down between us two," said the Teacher to the newly aroused man, "and let us reason together. You thought yourself a great reasoner, did you not, when you walked the Earth as So-and-so?"

"I did."

"You see that you were mistaken in your reasoning," the Teacher went on, "for you certainly passed through death, and you are now alive."

"But where am I?" He looked about him in a bewildered way. "Where am I, and who are you?"

"You are in eternity," replied the Teacher, "where you always have been and always will be."

"And you?"

"I am one who knows the workings of the Law."

"What law?"

"The law of rhythm, which drives the soul into and out of gross matter, as it drives the tides of the ocean into flood and ebb, and the consciousness of man into sleeping and waking."

"And it was you who awakened me? Are you, then, this law of rhythm?"

The Teacher smiled.

"I am not the law," he said, "but I am bound by it, even as you, save as I am temporarily able to transcend it by my will - again, even as you."

I caught my breath at the profundity of this simple answer, but the man seemed not to observe its significance. Even as he! Why, this man by his misdirected will had been able temporarily to transcend the law of immortality, even as the Teacher by his wisely directed will transcended the mortal in himself! My soul sang within me at this glimpse of the godlike possibilities of the human mind.

Sleeping Survivors.

"How long have I been asleep?" demanded the man
"In what year did you die?" the Teacher asked.
"In the year 1817."
"And the present year is known, according to the Christian calendar, as the year 1912. You have lain in a death-like sleep for ninety-five years."
"And was it really you who awakened me?"
"Yes."
"Why did you do it?"
"Because it suited my good pleasure," was the Teacher's rather stern reply. "It was not because you deserved to be awakened."
"And how long would I have slept if you had not aroused me?"
"I cannot say. Probably until those who had started even with you had left you far behind on the road of evolving life. Perhaps for centuries, perhaps for ages."
"You have taken a responsibility upon yourself," said the man.
"You do not need to remind me of that," replied the Teacher. "I weighed in my own mind the full responsibility and decided to assume it for a purpose of my own. For will is free."
"Yet you overpowered my will."
"I did; but by my own more potent will, more potent because wisely directed and backed by a greater energy."
"And what are you going to do with me?"
"I am going to assume the responsibility of your training."
"My training?"
"Yes."
"And you will make things easy for me?"
"On the contrary, I shall make things very hard for you; but you cannot escape my teaching."
"Shall you instruct me personally?"
"Personally in the sense that I will place you under the instruction of an advanced pupil of my own."
"Who? This man here?" he pointed to me.
"No. He is better occupied. I will take you to your teacher presently."
"And what will he show me?"

Is Reincarnation an Illusion?

> *"The panorama of immortality. And when you have learned the lesson so that you can never forget nor escape it, you will have to go back to the Earth and teach it to others; you will have to convert as many men to the truth of immortality as you have in the past deluded and misled by your false doctrines of materialism and death."*
> *"And what if I refuse? You have said that will is free."*
> *"Do you refuse?"*
> *"No, but what if I had?"*
> *"Then, instead of growing and developing under the law of action and reaction, which in the East they call karma, you would have been its victim."*
> *"I do not understand you."*
> *"He is indeed a wise man,"* said the Teacher, *"who understands the law of karma, which is also the law of cause and effect. But come. I will now take you to your new instructor."*
> Then, leaving me alone, the Teacher and his charge disappeared into the grey distance. I remained there a long time, pondering what I had seen and heard.[80]

This story illustrates quite clearly that those folk who are adamant during this life, that there is no life after death, and go around sharing and teaching that belief, almost get their most fervent wish. In fact, if you read what the teacher has to say, it does seem that those who consciously desire annihilation will be annihilated. I gather there are exceptions for those of unsound mind, and some sources say we are all considered to be unsound.

The Urantia book has more to say:

> **Sleeping Survivors.** *All mortals of survival status, in the custody of personal guardians of destiny, pass through the portals of natural death and, on the third period, personalize on the mansion worlds. Those accredited beings who have, for any reason, been unable to attain that level of intelligence mastery and endowment of spirituality which would entitle them to personal guardians, cannot thus immediately and directly go to the*

---

[80] *"Letters from a living dead man,"* Letter 39, The Doctrine of Death, page 154.

Sleeping Survivors.

mansion worlds. Such surviving souls must rest in unconscious sleep until the judgment day of a new epoch, a new dispensation, the coming of a Son of God to call the rolls of the age and adjudicate the realm, and this is the general practice throughout all Nebadon. It was said of Christ Michael that, when he ascended on high at the conclusion of his work on Earth, "He led a great multitude of captives." And these captives were the sleeping survivors from the days of Adam to the day of the Master's resurrection on Urantia.

The passing of time is of no moment to sleeping mortals; they are wholly unconscious and oblivious to the length of their rest. On reassembly of personality at the end of an age, those who have slept five thousand years will react no differently than those who have rested five days. Aside from this time delay these survivors pass on through the ascension regime identically with those who avoid the longer or shorter sleep of death.[81]

Later on, as I was reviewing "Astral Travel," I realized that they too reported in out-of-body travel that spirits seemed to be asleep. When I originally read this, I simply discarded it, because all other reports indicate that spirits may rest, but have no need of sleep – save for new arrivals. New arrivals do indeed often need to sleep as opposed to just resting, but once that phase is over, spirits no longer require sleep. I just assumed that out-of-body reports perhaps were less reliable than other ways of gathering information. Since out-of-body trips are of short duration, even sometimes only minutes long, and typically perhaps about 30 minutes, these individuals were not in any position to discover that these sleeping spirits do not wake up. Or not for a great many years, in any event.

> *Sleep time – You will occasionally notice newly arrived spirits who seem to be dormant or sleeping. This is because they do not realize that sleep is unnecessary in the astral here-now.*[82]

---

[81] *The Urantia Book*, Paper 30, part 4, page 341.
[82] *Astral Travel*, by Gavin and Yvonne Frost, published by Samuel Weiser, Inc. ISBN 0-87728-336-2, page 110.

Is Reincarnation an Illusion?

The explanation given here is certainly not impossible, but it is far more likely that these are simply sleeping survivors. Now if you believe in reincarnation, the idea that some folk may sleep for a thousand or more years before awakening does not sit well. It is a serious interruption to the idea of continuous growth. It really does challenge the idea of returning to work out karma and develop new skills, and have new experiences. But, you might have noticed that the teacher did not see this as an impediment to rebirth. Perhaps if he was aware of the comment in The Urantia Book that these folk have to sleep till the end of a dispensation, and that the first dispensation lasted from Adam and Eve till Pentecost, and that the second dispensation has not concluded, he might have had a different view. If we are meant to learn on Earth, then there is no point to the concept of sleeping survivors. It's just a serious road-block.

But before leaving this topic, I think it's as well to reflect on what we have here in this Chapter. We find an individual who has been asleep for a hundred years after death, by virtue of his very strong belief during his lifetime, that there is no life after death. He could however have so remained for over one thousand years - all because of a false belief that was very firmly held. Are there any other ramifications that might befall you or I because of beliefs that we hold fervently to? Actually, I believe there are, and in fact one with far more serious consequences. One that might specifically befall anyone who refuses to give up a belief in reincarnation. This is described in Chapter 16. But I think the greater message in this Chapter is that it is unwise to ever slam the door belief-wise. Be 99% sure, but if you are ever 100% sure and wrong, I think these sorts of pitfalls might well impede your journey.

Chapter 10

Non-survivors of death.

Of course it is utterly impossible from this side of the veil to prove that anyone might not survive death. It's hard enough dealing with proof of survival, and I guess you would not be reading this unless you already accept that. But how do you prove that anyone simply does not exist anymore? Well, I think one must accept that we can't. The only book I have come across that makes that assertion, is the Urantia Book.

> ***Spiritual (soul) death.*** *If and when mortal man has finally rejected survival, when he has been pronounced spiritually insolvent, morontially bankrupt, in the conjoint opinion of the Adjuster and the surviving seraphim, when such co-ordinate advice has been recorded on Uversa, and after the Censors and their reflective associates have verified these findings, thereupon do the rulers of Orvonton order the immediate release of the indwelling Monitor. But this release of the Adjuster in no way affects the duties of the personal or group seraphim concerned with that Adjuster-abandoned individual. This kind of death is final in its significance irrespective of the temporary continuation of the living energies of the physical and mind mechanisms. From the cosmic standpoint the mortal is already dead; the continuing life merely indicates the persistence of the material momentum of cosmic energies.*[83]

And again:

> *The technique of justice demands that personal or group guardians shall respond to the dispensational roll call in behalf of all nonsurviving personalities. The Adjusters of such nonsurvivors do not return, and when the rolls are called, the seraphim respond, but the*

---
[83] *The Urantia Book*, Paper 112, Part 3 page 1230.

Is Reincarnation an Illusion?

> *Adjusters make no answer. This constitutes the "resurrection of the unjust," in reality the formal recognition of the cessation of creature existence. This roll call of justice always immediately follows the roll call of mercy, the resurrection of the sleeping survivors. But these are matters which are of concern to none but the supreme and all-knowing Judges of survival values. Such problems of adjudication do not really concern us.*[84]

Sadly no real detail is given as to who these folks are who don't make it. Subsequent queries have revealed that some really evil folk are so evil that it is known that they will never ask for forgiveness. And, as a result they may be deemed spiritually dead, and their Indwelling Spirit may depart before they reach physical death. From an eternal perspective, these folks are already dead. We gather only a small number of folk fall into this category. As far as I am aware, Hitler survived, and certainly Judas did too. So did a number of Roman Emperors, including Julius Caesar and Constantine. But if this is the case, it surely shatters the concept of an eternal circle of life, returning time and again to correct that which we got wrong. Here is the claim that there are some individuals who simply terminate. But of course, as I said earlier, this is pretty much impossible to prove. Food for thought though?

---

[84] *The Urantia Book*, Paper 113, Part 6, page 1247.

Chapter 11

Hell.

As I suggested earlier, the concept of an eternal hell and reincarnation is totally incompatible. But what about the existence of a non-eternal hell? Well if hell is related to Karmic debt, then again it makes no sense to believe in both. A great number of "Light Workers" do not believe in the existence of a hell. Many of these folk say that they can only perceive love on the other side. Well that may well be true. The existence of "hell" does not mean an absence of love. From what I understand, hell is in fact simply a place or places where souls that are less "pure" are in harmony. They would not be in harmony in other places called heaven, because of the way they think. It is not a question of the absence of love, nor is it a place of punishment. On the other hand, it may not be nice for most folks to live in these places, but it suits the inhabitants. But it would be wrong to assume that the spirits who inhabit these dark places manifest much love for themselves or others.

Judge David Hatch, reports on the existence of hells:

> *There are horrors out here–far worse than the horrors on Earth. The decay from vice and intemperance is much worse here than there. I have seen faces and forms that were really frightful, faces that seemed to be half-decayed and falling in pieces. These are the hopeless cases, which even the League of workers I spoke about leave to their fate. It is uncertain what the fate of such people will be; whether they will reincarnate or not in this cycle, I do not know.*[85]

And later, in Letter 18:

---

[85] Edited out of *"Letters from the Light,"* but found in the original, *"Letters from a living dead man"* in Letter 11.

Is Reincarnation an Illusion?

> *Some time ago I told you of my intention to visit hell; but when I began investigations on that line there proved to be many hells.*
>
> *Each man who is not content with the orthodox hell of fire and brimstone builds one out of the mind stuff suited to his imaginative need.*
>
> *I believe that men place themselves in hell, that no God puts them there. I began looking for a hell of fire and brimstone, and found it. Dante must have seen the same things I saw.*
>
> *But there are other and individual hells*[86]

Continued again in Letter 36:

> *You must know that there are many hells, and they are mostly of our own making. That is one of those platitudes, which are based upon fact.*
>
> *Desiring one day to see the particular kind of hell to which a drunkard would be likely to go, I sought that part of the hollow sphere around the world*[87] *which corresponds to one of those countries where drunkenness is most common. Souls, when they come out, usually remain in the neighbourhood where they have lived, unless there is some strong reason to the contrary.*
>
> *I had no difficulty in finding a hell full of drunkards. What do you fancy they were doing? Repenting their sins? Not at all. They were hovering around those places on Earth where the fumes of alcohol, and the heavier fumes of those who over-indulge in alcohol, made sickening the atmosphere. It is no wonder that sensitive people dislike the neighbourhood of drinking saloons.*
>
> *You would draw back with disgust and refuse to write for me should I tell you all that I saw. One or two instances will suffice.*
>
> *I placed myself in a sympathetic and neutral state, so that I could see into both worlds.*
>
> *A young man with restless eyes and a troubled face entered one of those "gin palaces" in which gilding and*

---

[86] *"Letters from a living dead man"*, Letter 18, page 55.
[87] This is a reference to the Astral Plane and is not in fact any part of the hells.

> *highly polished imitation mahogany tend to impress the miserable wayfarer with the idea that he is enjoying the luxury of the "kingdoms of this world." The young man's clothes were threadbare, and his shoes had seen much wear. A stubble of beard was on his chin, for the price of a shave is the price of a drink, and a man takes that which he desires most – when he can get it.*
>
> *He was leaning on the bar, drinking a glass of some soul-destroying compound.*
>
> *And close to him, taller than he and bending over him, with its repulsive, bloated, ghastly face pressed close to his, as if to smell his whiskey-tainted breath, was one of the most horrible astral beings, which I have seen in this world since I came out. The hands of the creature (and I use that word to suggest its vitality) - the hands of the creature were clutching the young man's form, one long and naked arm was around his shoulders, the other around his hips. It was literally sucking the liquor-soaked life of its victim, absorbing him, using him, in the successful attempt to enjoy vicariously the passion which death had intensified.*
>
> *But was that a creature in hell you ask? Yes, for I could look into its mind and see its sufferings. Forever (the words "forever" may be used of that which seems endless) this entity was doomed to crave and crave and never to be satisfied.*[88]

This story is consistent with what James Padgett channeled, save only that this particular event takes place in the Astral Plane, which is unfortunately accessible to those whose real home is in another dimension – the lowest part of the Spirit Spheres. This obsessive behavior is attempted by evil spirits in order to satisfy their cravings for alcohol, and the result of this behavior will eventually lead to the entity falling even lower in the hells.

James Padgett has many reports of spirits in hell, some of whom were his own colleagues and associates from the legal profession. (No comment required.)

---

[88] *"Letters from a living dead man"*, Letter 36, page 136.

Is Reincarnation an Illusion?

> *I am a spirit, who cannot tell you of the joys of heaven, but I can describe the horrors of hell, for just as these other spirits described to you their homes of beauty and happiness, I can describe my home of ugliness and torment. Do you wish me to do so?*
>
> *Well know then, that when I lived on Earth I was a man of very considerable intellectual powers and acquirements and also of an intense animal nature, so much so, that it overcame my judgment and what moral qualities I had, and I became at last a slave to my appetites which were varied, especially my appetite for drink. I had many friends of position, social and otherwise, and I was considered a brilliant newspaper writer, and had access to the inner political circles that were then in control of the government.*
>
> *My weakness, or rather the effect of the strength of my animal nature, was known to many of my friends, and they, in many ways, tried to help me and rescue me from my evil and destructive course of living, and, at times, I would succeed in reforming my conduct; but, alas, not for any great length of time; when I would again relapse into my deplorable habits and become the controlled victim of my destroying appetites.*
>
> *Of course human friendship and sympathy had their limits, and finally my friends gave me up as lost and past redemption, and I surely and quickly sunk lower and lower in my moral condition, and at last, died a drunkard, unwept and unsung except for the evil that I had done. It was undoubtedly a relief to my friends and acquaintances when I passed over, and forever relieved them of the shadow of my presence and the ghost of what I had been.*
>
> *But such was my end, and when I came to the spirit world I found that I still was deserted by friends who had become spirits before me, except some who liked the flowing bowl as I did on Earth, and who were inhabitants of the unattractive place that I found myself in when my habitation became fixed.*
>
> *I never, when on Earth, thought much of the future life, except to convince myself that there was no hell, and if there was a God He was not bothered about me, a mere man of many millions.*

Hell.

But oh, the fatal mistake; and the unexpected realization of the fact that there is a hell! Whether there is a God I don't know, for I have never seen him or felt his influence. But since I came to you tonight, and heard the messages of those two spirits who described their wonderful homes and their condition of happiness, and ascribed them all to the kindness and care of God, I have commenced to think that there may be a God, and that my mistake was greater than I have heretofore realized. But this is a digression from what I started out to write.

That there is a hell, I know to my sorrow and sufferings, for I have been the occupant of one for oh these many years; and it is always the same place of horrors and darkness, except sometime it is lighted by the flame of lurid light that comes from the anger and sufferings of some unfortunate like myself.

In this hell of mine, and there are many like it, instead of beautiful homes, as the other spirits described, we have dirty, rotten hovels all crooked and decayed, with all the foul smells of a charnel house ten times intensified, and instead of beautiful lawns and green meadows and leafy woods filled with musical birds making the echoes ring with their songs, we have barren wastes, and holes of darkness and gloom and the cries and cursings of spirits of damnation without hope; and instead of living, silvery waters we have stagnant pools filled with all kinds of repulsive reptiles and vermin, and smells of inexpressible, nauseating stinks.

I tell you that these are all real, and not creatures of the imagination or the outflowing of bitter recollections. And as for love, it has never shown its humanizing face in all the years that I have been here - only cursings and hatred and bitter scathings and imprecations, and grinning spirits with their witchlike cacklings. No rest, no hope, no kind words or ministering hand to wipe away the scalding tears which so often flow in mighty volumes. No, hell is real and hell is here.

We do not have any fire and brimstone, or grinning devils with pitch forks and hoofs and horns as the churches teach; but what is the need or necessity for such accompaniments? They would not add to the horrors or to

131

Is Reincarnation an Illusion?

> our torments. I tell you my friend that I have faintly described our homes in these infernal regions and I cannot picture them as they are.
> But the horror and pity of it all is that hope does not come to us with one faint smile to encourage us that there may at some time be an ending to all these torments, and in our hopeless despair we realize that our doom is fixed for all eternity.
> As the rich man in hell said, if I could only send Lazarus to tell my poor, erring brothers on Earth of what awaits them, how gladly I would do so and save their souls from the eternal torment.
> Well, I have written you a long letter and am tired, because it is the first time that I have attempted to write for many long years, and I find some difficulty in gathering my thoughts so as to be able to write in an intelligent and collected manner. So I must stop.[89]

Even Sylvia Browne says there is a hell. But her hell is rather different. Hers is just a bad trip, a virtual tour through a bad place. This is what Sylvia says:

> When a person on The Dark Side dies, their spirit never experiences the tunnel and the sacred light at its end. Instead, they immediately go through The Other Side's Left Door, or as my six-year-old granddaughter Angelia calls it, Mean Heaven. I know this implies that when we reach The Other Side we see two doors and choose between the left and the right. But only on very, very rare occasions is anyone conscious of seeing two doors, and it never happens to someone who's headed for the Right Door. There's no danger of a spirit going through the wrong door by accident and ending up where they don't belong. The vast majority of us are propelled straight to our appropriate destination with no awareness of doors at all.[90]

She goes on to add:

---
[89] A spirit describes his experience in one of the hells. https:// new-birth.net/link10/ received January 5th, 1916 by James Padgett.
[90] *Life on the Other Side*, page 66.

Hell.

> *Every living spirit, including those on The Dark Side, is a child of God and loved by him unconditionally, whether that love is returned or not. And God will not allow any of his children to be doomed to The Dark Side's horseshoe cycle for an eternity. Just as the spirits on The Other Side eventually bring ghosts Home, they also, in an act of courage and compassion that may take hundreds of years, will finally manage to catch a dark spirit in that moment before it reaches the Left Door and absorb it into the healing peace of God's light where it belongs.*[91]

Well, there are a lot of differences in this tale, but at least Sylvia agrees there are dark places. To give Sylvia due credit, she has discovered for herself yet another dark place, and I guess she has not yet really integrated this place into her overall concept, because I find her explanation rather unsatisfactory. Of this "different hell" which she calls the Holding Place, she says:

> *The Holding Place is kind of an anteroom to the Godless darkness behind the Left Door, separate from it but too close to be completely isolated from its pervasive negativity. The residents of the Holding Place are the heartbroken, heart-breaking despair suicides, and those other spirits who spend their lives on this Earth in that grey area between The Dark Side and the divine light of God. Their behavior toward themselves and the rest of humanity reflects the confusion of their faith in and relationship to God. The desolate souls in the Holding Place can still make a choice about whether to proceed on through the Left Door and horseshoe back for another incarnation, or to move on to The Other Side. The key, as always, is God.*[92]

We have news of one of the most famous spirits in Christianity – Judas. Judas tells of his life in hell:

---

[91] *Life on The Other Side*, page 67.
[92] *Life on The Other Side*, page 69.

As you will remember, last time I told you how the spirit who accompanied me, informed me that the time had come for leaving this entrance place into the spirit world. I had come to understand perfectly well that I lived no longer on Earth, I had even arrived at the knowledge, that my "physical" state, that is, the condition of my spiritual body, was horrible. It was ugly, and I felt very bad.

The spirit took me by my hand and led me to a very different place, at the same speed as he had taken me from the place of my death to the spirit world. Now I want you to describe what you are seeing.

[H.. It seemed as if I was standing at the top of a mountain or hill. Below I could see a pretty valley, with forests, meadows, springs and streams. I heard birds singing, it was like a beautiful summer day. Suddenly, everything began to dry off. The green colors turned brown, the leaves fell off the trees, and after a short time, I saw a disastrous landscape. Everything was dry, the Earth cracked, a few trunks like skeletons without life, the streams had disappeared, leaving behind only their stony beds. There was no sunshine anymore, everything seemed dark, like a winter dawn in the northern regions, but without snow, and the silence of death reigned.]

What a contrast! Well, this is how the place looked like, where the spirit took me. There he left me, saying that I could find an abandoned house, and that there I would have to live, until I had the capacity to leave that place.

You think that it was horrible, but I tell you frankly, I didn't find this so bad in the beginning. I met with many spirits in my own condition, I got used to the little light and the barren landscape, but eventually I almost despaired. The negativity, so much negativity in those spirits! I had always been a cheerful person, I liked to joke, to sing, to dance, but at this place, in this hell, there was no singing or dancing, neither laughter nor a single word of comfort. Everybody took care of his own business, there was not much communication, there was not much to do, nothing to read, nothing to write, only thinking. And there were no children.

And my memories came, good and bad memories, but mainly the recollection of my betrayal of the Master and of my suicide. I don't know which one was worse.

One day, one of my taciturn neighbors broke his silence and told me that Jesus had visited this place some short time ago. He had told them that there was hope for them, that they could leave this place, and that further on a better world was waiting for them. But very few paid attention to him.

When I heard this, I really broke down. Maybe there was hope, yes, but not for me. I had caused Jesus' death, of that luminous spirit, as the neighbor described him to me. What could I do? Nothing but to be resigned.

I also found out that there were better places, which I could visit, and I did so. I found places very similar to Earth, with more light, much more light than where I lived, and the spirits were better, that is to say, they looked better, they treated me well in spite of my ugliness, but I simply didn't belong there, I had to return.[93]

Now in the subsequent 150 odd messages Judas gives remarkable descriptions of the rest of the heavens, and there seems very little doubt that things are as he claims – that he was able to progress out of the hells into the highest of the heavens. And he has never claimed to have reincarnated in the 2000 years he has been in spirit.

I recently came across two books dating from 1914, by the same author that have remarkable descriptions of the hells. This is because the tale is told of "The Officer" a fellow who got into darkness, and managed to dig himself ever deeper, before changing, and asking God to help him get out. This book is called "Gone West", and the author is J.S.M. Ward. The second book mostly deals with the Officer's experiences in the Astral Plane, and is called "A Subaltern in Spirit Land."

---

[93] Judas' experience of the hells. https://new-birth.net/link11/ received by H. on September 6th, 2001

Is Reincarnation an Illusion?

I should, to be fair, point out that a book I used to support the concept of Sleeping Survivors asserts there is no hell. This was "Astral Travel." So I had better quote that:

> *Notice that in Figure 6.1 no downward direction is indicated. In analysis of reports from hundreds of subjects we have found only two that discussed a downward-into-hell experience. We believe that these two subjects created this hell-like reality for themselves, probably because they had been so strongly imprinted with the idea of hell from fundamentalist Christian parents.*[94]

Well, the point here may be simply word usage. We certainly have had angels tell us that no-where in all of God's creation are there places such as those described as hell in the Bible. But there are lots of un-developed and evil spirits none the less. And they live in places that give them no happiness. In fact, "Astral Travel" goes to a great deal of effort to explain the need for psychic protection from presumably these very same homeless spirits. The details cover many pages of instructions. They even say, in capitals:

DO NOT MEDITATIVELY ASTRAL TRAVEL WITHOUT PSYCHIC PROTECTION.[95]

And they follow this warning with a long paragraph about the fact that they know what they are talking about. So where do these dangerous entities live, if there is no hell? Perhaps I could invent a new name, and call it no-hell? The hell you're having when you're not in hell?

Now, if hell exists, no matter what you call it, there is no point to the idea of Karmic debt being paid out on Earth. Quite simply, if your actions on Earth can lead to your spending time in dark and unpleasant places, until you have changed, then the whole idea of Karma being played out in a second Earth life is not realistic. And if spirits can progress in spirit, way beyond that point at which they entered the next world, the whole basis of reincarnation begins to look very shaky. In fact we will talk about progress in the spheres as a topic all by itself.

---

[94] *Astral Travel*, page 109.
[95] *Astral Travel*, page 73.

And there is yet another aspect to consider. The hell that I have found, can be exited, and is exited by changing and growing into a different person. This is simply the beginning of potentially massive spiritual growth. Why stop this pattern to return to earth and face a possible serious regression, because you can't remember any lessons from the life you have lived?

Chapter 12

Getting out of Hell.

Whether it was the plight of his lawyer friends, or simply altruism, James Padgett developed a real knack for getting spirits to progress rapidly out of darkness. He dedicated one day a week to talking to these desperate spirits, and it took no time at all for him to have a very long list of spirits pleading for help. Many of their tales have been published, and in a few cases, there is a before and afterwards message, when the spirit comes back to record his progress. He helped some famous spirits, and this is when one realizes that even if one's sojourn is not eternal, it certainly can be a very long time indeed. Julius Caesar first makes contact on September 16th, 1915.[96] At that stage he had been in darkness 2040 years, by my reckoning. But by May 1st, 1917 he has reached the Third Spirit Sphere - beyond where most folks first arrive in spirit. An explanation of this is contained in Chapter 16.

There are other spirits less well known, but no less impressive cases too. His old lawyer friend Edwin Forrest first made contact in June 27th, 1916, and by February 27th, 1917 he is out of darkness.[97]

An interesting passage is found in "30 Years among the Dead," when a spirit is first awakened, and sees for the first time the condition of its spirit body. It is quite upset at how "homely" it appears. One needs to know the word homely had a far more unattractive meaning in the 1920's. This is another long transcript, very similar to others, and the remarks about the appearance of the spirit have been set in bold, so that you can skim to that if preferred.

---

[96] Julius Caesar writes that Earthly position does not determine one's spiritual abode. https://new-birth.net/link12/ received by James Padgett on September 16th, 1915.
[97] Forrest writes that he is out of darkness and in the light of Love – https://new-birth.net/link13/ received by James Padgett on February 27th, 1917.

Is Reincarnation an Illusion?

EXPERIENCE, OCTOBER 27, 1919

Spirit: **MRS. SIMONS**   *Patient:* **MRS. SR**
Psychic: **MRS. WICKLAND**

The controlling entity groaned and immediately placed hands on back, apparently in great pain.

Doctor.	Are you in trouble? Have you lost your body without understanding it?
Spirit.	I don't know.
Dr.	We can relieve your pain. Tell us who you are.
Sp.	I don't know.
Dr.	Surely you know your own name.
Sp.	I cannot think.
Dr.	How long have you been dead?
Sp.	I don't know if I am dead.
Dr.	What did your friends call you?
Sp.	Mrs. Simons.
Dr.	Where did you live?
Sp.	Chicago.
Dr.	Where did you live in Chicago?
Sp.	It's a long time ago, and I don't know. I have not felt just right.
Dr.	In what way?
Sp.	I felt so small, and was so uncomfortable.
Dr.	Do you realize that you were interfering with some one?
Sp.	I know that I am in such a stupor. I don't feel natural.
Dr.	Do you know the reason for that?
Sp.	No.
Dr.	You did not believe in spirits, did you?
Sp.	No, and I don't believe it yet.
Dr.	Then you do not believe in your own self, do you? You thought anyone who believed in spirits was foolish. Is it not foolish to be an Earthbound spirit? Do you realize that you have been one?
Mrs. Sr.	Do you know me?
Sp.	I know that voice; it belongs to a friend of mine.

Getting out of Hell.

Dr. Where is she?
Sp. In Chicago.
Dr. What was her business?
Sp. I don't know. Everything is so dark and I cannot remember anything. I know that voice, but I cannot tell you who it belongs to. I cannot remember her name at all, but I knew her in Chicago. She used to call and see me. My friend was always like sunshine to me. She helped me.
Dr. What did she do?
Sp. She always came with such a nice cheerful disposition, but she got interested in Spiritualism once. I told her not to bother with it because there was nothing in it. I would not have anything to do with that.
I miss her so. I only see her once in a while. I feel so little and uncomfortable. To save my life I cannot think of her name.
Dr. What was her first name?
Sp. It comes to me now! It was R. Something ails my memory and things are so queer to me. Once in a while I get a glimpse of light, then I feel I am locked up in a small place. You know I am a big woman and in that little place (aura of patient) I was so crowded that I had no feeling.
Dr. Did you get warmed up occasionally?
Sp. Yes, once in a while. I do not know what is the matter, but something burns me sometimes. (Static treatment given patient.) Now it is all dark, dark. I do not see a thing. I do not know which is the best, the fire, or being crowded so that I got no breath. I could not breathe. I do not know why it is. But I seemed to have gotten a shock.
Dr. Did you die from a shock?
Sp. I cannot tell that I am dead because I do not feel dead. I have had fire, and sometimes it was like thunder, shooting pain.
Mrs. Sr. Do you remember Dr. Wickland?
Sp. Yes.

141

Is Reincarnation an Illusion?

Mrs. Sr.	Do you remember that machine he had?
Sp.	The one that shot fire?
Mrs. Sr.	Yes, and that is the fire you feel.
Sp.	Why, I didn't take treatments from him.
Mrs. Sr.	You have been bothering me all these years.
Sp.	Why did I bother you?
Mrs. Sr.	Have Doctor explain it to you.
Dr.	It is not hard to explain. You are now a spirit and have been hovering around your friend. That is why you feel uncomfortable. You are not in Chicago now, you are in California. You are in Los Angeles, California. Don't you remember Mrs. Sr?
Sp.	Yes, she was in Chicago.
Dr.	You are both in Los Angeles now.
Sp.	I was in Chicago. I always had pains in my legs, and very often in my head.
Mrs. S.	You gave me those pains lately.
Dr.	You loaned Mrs. Sr. your pains.
Sp.	No, you are mistaken in that.
Mrs. Sr.	Do you remember Mrs. Wickland of Chicago - Dr. Wickland's wife? Do you remember she was a psychic?
Sp.	I don't seem to remember. It is strange I don't know anything.
Mrs. Sr.	You thought you knew so much.
Sp.	I supposed I knew. You meddled with that foolish thing, Spiritualism, and I did not want to have anything to do with it. Have you been fooling with it again?
Mrs. Sr.	No, you have been fooling with me.
Sp.	No, I did not want to have anything to do with that; there is nothing in it. I didn't like that fire - I could not stand it. It chased me away. I suffered terribly. When I was chased out I was locked up in a new room.
Dr.	You were locked up in a room of ignorance.
Mrs. Sr.	It is a long time since you died.
Sp.	I am not dead.

Getting out of Hell.

Dr.	Look at this hand. Is that yours? You are using another body now. You are proving that what you thought was humbug is true.
Mrs. Sr.	Do you know what year it is Mrs. Simons?
Sp.	I don't know anything. Where is my home? Where is my girl?
Mrs. Sr.	Your girl is not here. You are in Los Angeles, California.
Sp.	No, now you are a little off. Mrs. Sr., don't you know you are in Chicago?
Mrs. Sr.	I have been here in California for six and one-half years.
Sp.	We are in Chicago. Such a foolish woman! She is hypnotized and wants to have me believe such a story.
Dr.	Wouldn't you like to understand matters? You have been dead a good many years, and were hovering around your friend, Mrs. Sr. You were driven away from her by electricity. Now you are allowed to control my wife's body temporarily so you may acquire understanding. Do you know anything about the purpose of life? Did that ever interest you? No, therefore you think there could not be anything in a higher life. You call yourself Mrs. Simons. This body belongs to Mrs. Wickland and she is in Los Angeles, California. You claim you are in Chicago and we cannot convince you of the facts. You have been obsessing Mrs. Sr.
Sp.	I came to her because it was so dark. It seems I had been sleeping for a while, then I woke up. I saw a light, then I was here. I could see just a little light if I could be with her.
Dr.	You got into her magnetic aura and made her suffer. In order to get you out I applied electricity to her.
Mrs. Sr.	Do you know what I told Doctor? I told him to give you that electricity.
Sp.	You have no sympathy for a poor old, lady like me.

Is Reincarnation an Illusion?

Dr.   Would you have liked to have an Earthbound spirit control your body?

Sp.   I will not listen to you.

Dr.   You are willing to bother your friend.

Sp.   I do not know whether I have been bothering her. I have only been around her to see light.

Dr.   Then how did you happen to get the electricity when I gave it to her? I have never treated you.

Mrs. Sr.   By right you ought to pay Dr. Wickland for that treatment, Mrs. Simons.

Sp.   Tell me one thing - how did I come here? I do not think you are right, Mrs. Sr., but if you should be, how did you come to California?

Mrs. Sr.   By paying my railroad fare I came here. Did you pay anything?

Sp.   I never paid anything, so how did I get here? I don't believe it anyhow - you cannot say that to me! I am in Chicago, and Mrs. Sr. was never in California.

Dr.   Do you hear that rumble? That is a train leaving Los Angeles for Chicago.

Sp.   That is the Northwestern train.

Dr.   There is no Northwestern out here. What do you gain by arguing? When you understand the situation you will appreciate what I am trying to tell you.
What would you think of a person who refused to understand life, who has been dead seven or eight years, whose body is lost and in the grave, and who is an ignorant spirit, bothering one who was formerly a friend?

Sp.   I cannot see how that is.

Dr.   We are telling you facts.

Mrs. Sr.   Your body was buried in Waltheim Cemetery six or eight years ago.

Sp.   I have been sleeping. I woke up with very severe pains and I could not move very well, and I felt so crowded.

Dr.   That was because Mrs. Sr.'s body is smaller than yours, and you have been obsessing her.

Getting out of Hell.

Sp.	*How could I get in that body? I felt I could hardly move. I have to find out what you are talking about. I don't believe it. I want to know what object you have to say such things?*
Dr.	*Did you ever study Life at all?*
Sp.	*I studied trees and Nature.*
Dr.	*Did you ever observe how the tree grows? It is wonderful. God puts life into it and it grows. What is life?*
Sp.	*God, I suppose.*
Dr.	*Have you ever seen mind?*
Sp.	*Mind is mind.*
Dr.	*Have you ever seen mind?*
Sp.	*No, you could not talk if you had no mind.*
Dr.	*Mind is invisible, isn't it?*
Sp.	*I haven't seen it.*
Dr.	*Suppose we tell you that you are invisible to us. When I speak to you I can see only my wife's body.*
Sp.	*Your wife's body? Mrs. Sr., what is the matter? Have I lost my body?*
Mrs. Sr.	*Yes, you have.*
Dr.	*Only your stubbornness keeps you in the dark.*
Sp.	*I haven't seen or heard anything. There was a time, I tell you, when I walked on and on, but always in the dark, and it seemed like I never could get there. I rested, then I kept on walking. At first I could see just a little light, and it seems like it came to me in a flash - "Mrs. Sr.!" I thought, "Yes, she was a friend of mine" and then I could see her.*
Dr.	*You transferred yourself by thought.*
Sp.	*Then I had a terrible pain. I thought I had lost all my pain for a little while. I woke up and felt no pain at first, but when I got to that light all the pain came back.*
Dr.	*You had pain when you had your body. You must understand you are a spirit, invisible to us. When an Earthbound spirit comes in touch with a mortal body he again has the pains he*

	passed out with. You got in touch with Mrs. Sr., and had your mortal pains again.
	You have caused trouble. You were selfish and you have not gained anything by it. In the spirit world you will have to serve others. Realize that you are now a spirit; you no longer have a physical body. Why did you not become a tree as you expected to?
Mrs. Sr.	*Your body is buried in Waltheim Cemetery, Chicago. Go to the cemetery and see if you have a tombstone there.*
Sp.	*I don't want to go and examine my tombstone in the cemetery.*
Dr.	*Did you go to church?*
Sp.	*I believed that when I died there was nothing more. I didn't want to have such foolish thoughts as you had, Mrs. Sr. I had my own ideas and did not need yours.*
Dr.	*God created the world but you did not investigate anything.*
Sp.	*(In great excitement.) My God! My God I see my mother! Why, she is in her grave - yes, many years ago! It must be a ghost. She looks so beautiful.*
Dr.	*She did not limit her mind as you did. She did not want to be a tree. You must be willing to learn. Jesus said: "Except ye become as little children ye shall not enter into the kingdom of Heaven."*
Sp.	*(Of Jewish faith.) I do not believe in Jesus.*
Dr.	*What you believe, or what you do not believe, has nothing to do with the fact of life.*
Sp.	*Mother, is that really you? Why, look at that beautiful road, with beautiful trees and flowers! See that beautiful garden and those beautiful houses, and my mother walking around.*
Dr.	*Your mother is not a tree, is she?*
Sp.	*Now she is walking on that beautiful road. She says: "Come, this is my home." Her home, but not mine. Can't I go with my mother?*

Getting out of Hell.

Dr.   *Ignorance cannot enter the "Kingdom of Heaven."*

Sp.   *Look at that steep hill which I have to climb! I cannot climb that hill with the big body I have. Mother says: "No, you cannot climb it with your body, but you have to climb the hill of understanding, and you must forget yourself. Forget that you have existed in your selfishness. You must serve."*
I know; I. know. Yes, I was selfish. Mother, I will try, but help me! Help me up there! I cannot do it alone. (Crying.)
I cannot stay in this misery any longer! Take me, take me, Mother, with you. Take me with you and show me!
She says I must work and not be lazy as I was in life and expect everybody to do something for me. If they did not do what I wanted then I got angry.
My mother says: "Now you have to serve. You have to work to climb this hill of understanding to a higher life. You have now to learn the first lesson of life, the lesson of understanding, and you will have to go up that hill until you have gotten away from all selfishness, jealousy and envy. You must do that."
"You must also ask forgiveness for what you have done to your old friend. You will have to do it," my mother says. "You will have to be forgiven. (Crying.) No, you must ask for forgiveness, because you have been selfish, very selfish. All thoughts of self must be thrown away, and you must live for others. I am your mother, but I cannot take you to my home yet, because you must learn."
(Doubtfully.) She says she is my mother - but I do not know. Yes - I believe it must be, but she looks so beautiful.

Dr.   *That is because she is filled with the spirit of truth.*

Sp.	Mrs. Sr., if I ask you to forgive me, will you forgive me?
Mrs. Sr.	I surely will. You didn't know any better.
Sp.	You have helped me to light, and it was because of you that I reached this understanding.
Mrs. S.	You must thank the Wicklands for it.
Sp.	I don't feel like thanking them for it. Mother says I must, because I would still be in that terrible pain and agony but for them. She says I got into your magnetic aura with a mind full of pain and selfishness and envy. Love was not in me, except selfish love, and she says now I must have love for others and not self. Forget self and work for others, then, she says, I will be happy.
Dr.	"Love is the fulfillment of the law."
Sp.	I don't know. I didn't have much interest in those things. I now see myself as I was. I was a bundle of selfishness. Mrs. Sr., I must also ask you to forgive me because many times I spoke to you in a very rude way, and I was selfish. I felt people should always come to see me and they had to do it. I see now my selfishness. Mrs. Sr., please forgive me. I ask it now from my heart. I see now, but before I did not want to see it, because that was putting my past life before me, and how I had lived for self. **I do not want that evil, ugly, homely body of mine, which they (guiding intelligences) show me. That is not my body.**
Dr.	That is your spiritual body, for you have made no other. You have made a spiritual body of only selfishness and jealousy.
Sp.	**It is all crippled and wrinkled.**
Dr.	You will have to alter it by your good acts for others. You will have to wear the garment you made until you have earned another.
Sp.	**To think I should have to wear such an ugly, homely, old fool thing!** That - that spiritual body of mine - just because I did not do anybody any good!

Getting out of Hell.

Dr.   You will have to wear that and be happy until you have learned how to earn another, and to climb the hill of understanding and wisdom.

Sp.   So I have to live now in that awful body of mine. I have to get in.

Dr.   Serve - serve your fellow man.

Sp.   I will be brave, and I will try, because now I see what I should have done, but I did not do it. **They say it is not too late, and I will try to wear that body, all wrinkled and so homely. They tell me I can soon wear it out by good acts, and each time I do some good act, some wrinkles will be taken away, and there will be a change for the better.** I will try to be happy. It is hard. Mrs. Sr., help me!

Dr.   We will all help you.

Sp.   Give me some little sympathy because I have to be in that terrible, homely body of mine that I have made only by selfishness and hate. I will wear it until I can do better. I need help and strength so that I can stand it.

Mrs. Sr., forgive me. They say I have done harm to you, and that now I have to wear that homely body and have to serve you. I will serve you and help you. My first lesson will be how to be kind. I will, I will.

Dr.   You will find many good friends who will help you. Ask the intelligent spirits to help you. Will you ask them?

Sp.   Yes, I will. They say I must thank you for those thunder shots.

Dr.   Do you believe in spirits now?

Sp.   I must, I suppose. Don't be like I was, selfish, but do what you can so that you will not have to get into a crippled-up body like mine. They say, no one can help us to work out our own salvation. Make your spirit body more beautiful than mine.

Now I will go and begin my work. Goodbye.[98]

---

[98] *"30 Years Among the Dead"* by Dr Carl Wickland, page 254 -260

From this little tale we see that those spirits who are less developed, and are still carrying a lot of "karma", have unattractive spirit bodies. This is the condition of spirits in "hell" – homely, dark, wrinkled, crippled, and unattractive. As this is not the norm, it follows that there is a progression in spirit.

The issue of progress in spirit is also often refuted by believers in reincarnation. Mind you, not by all. But if progress is meant to occur on Earth, then how can we have progress in spirit? Or why? And if you progress fast in spirit, then why would you choose to reincarnate, if you can progress so fast in spirit? We will address this in the next chapter.

Chapter 13

Progress in spirit.

Well you might be pleased to hear that in six years in spirit my mother has reached the Seventh sphere, and has now passed through it. But I don't have a series of recorded messages that I can show you. But what I have discovered is that James Padgett's own wife, made it past the Seventh sphere in just one year. He was just an American lawyer, and an orthodox (Methodist) Christian until his wife passed away. He was so distraught that he sought the company of a medium, in the hope of making contact with her. Instead he was told he had the ability to receive messages himself, via automatic writing. So he tried. Initially he was not very successful, and then he had a break through. In the period 1914 to 1921 he delivered an enormous number of messages, probably well over 2500 - and this entirely ignores the communications from folks in the hells that he devoted a day a week to, and are believed to number 3,500. The originals of the messages still exist, in boxes, although they are starting to decay. But you can find the bulk of his messages on the web, as well as in various publications. One source of the publications is F.C.D.T. Publishing.[99] But the papers I will refer to are on the web. In fact they are all collated under one header page.[100] Helen Padgett's progress can be summarized as follows:

- First recorded message, May 31st, 1914.
- Talks of being in the Third spirit sphere, November 16th, 1914.
- Describes Fifth sphere transition, January 17th, 1915.
- Describes her transition to the First Celestial Sphere, March 3rd, 1915.

Of course this is very fast spiritual development, but, if you read Padgett you will discover why that is so. (Chapter 16 covers this very briefly.) Suffice it to say, that although my mother was initially not keen

---

[99] *Angelic Revelations of Divine Truth Volume 1* published by Foundation Church of Divine Truth, ISBN 1887621008
[100] Progressing and reaching Gold! https://new-birth.net/link14/

Is Reincarnation an Illusion?

on my explanations, because she died a staunch Catholic, she has now accepted them, and put into practice just what James Padgett suggested to his wife. With the same spectacular results.

Sylvia Browne raises an excellent point in her reasons why she believes in reincarnation. Since the Spirit Spheres are places of ever increasing goodness, how much real learning can occur there? In fact, this is how she puts it:

> As Francine once asked me, "What have you ever learned when times were good?" And times at Home aren't just good, they're idyllic. True, on The Other Side we can study every subject that exists, including negativity. But studying negativity without experiencing it, and gaining the strength and wisdom that result from overcoming it, is much like learning to drive a car by reading about it without ever getting behind the wheel, or believing you can perform brain surgery because you've memorized every available textbook on the subject. Since negativity doesn't exist on The Other Side, we come here to confront it, grow from it, and eventually defeat it, for the benefit of humankind, for ourselves, and for god. Whether it takes one incarnation or a hundred, we always keep our promise to our Creator, and He keeps his promise to us, that we will never settle for less than the finest expression of the gifts we've been given.[101]

Well, it's a good point, but if Sylvia really believes this, then she also believes that through all eternity Earth will not progress. It will always be in darkness. This is because if she believes we must reincarnate to learn, and learning must be in darkness, then Earth must always be dark. And of course, if Earth is dark, its inhabitants must on average be dark, so only a very small number of spirits can be expected to escape the cycle. If too many here were "advanced", then Earth would not be dark enough. This is a very serious catch 22 situation.

But, there is a truth to what Francine says, and I have found it hard to understand, never mind believe. Discerning Truth is apparently harder in spirit than here. That sounds frankly impossible, but one reason why

---

[101] *Life on The Other Side*, page 200.

Progress in Spirit.

we can discern truth here, is that you can stumble upon it. If you imagine a world where you are surrounded by others that are very similar in outlook, you will never be challenged. And even the teachers you have won't challenge you, unless you actually ask for that challenge.

The other reason why it can be so hard, is that folks literally live their truth, and can see enough personal growth and happiness to be sure they are on the right track. It does not seem to bother them that many others have different paths, yet apparently similar happiness. But back to the spiritual progress of the Earth.

The Urantia Book and many other sources, such as Padgett tell a different story. They all assure us that eventually Earth will reach what they call "Light and Life" – or Heaven-on-Earth. Now, if we reach that stage, and according to Sylvia Browne, folks are still reincarnating to experience negativity, what on Earth will they do?

But it is a very good point, because we already have spirit guides here who incarnated on other planets – planets settled in Light and Life – and they tell us that they are here to experience, albeit second hand, the trials and tribulations of a darkened planet. And, Sylvia is right, first hand is best, but if you only have one mortal existence, and your planet is settled in Light and Life, then the range of experiences you can come across are limited. Listen to Samuel on this very subject:

> "I'm with you my dear friend and student. My love and respect for you dwells in my heart, my mind and my soul. It is a blessing for me to be with you through good times and bad in this 'marker' of the twelfth year of our association, even though for the greater time of our liaison you remained oblivious to the source of this regular input.
>
> "Be assured that for us both all our time together has been of great value, as we each managed to progress in our age-long endeavor to eventually reach a state of total perfection. One could hardly imagine a greater contrast between our home worlds. For the likes of me, having grown up in an environment in the middle stages of Light and Life, it is an amazing learning experience to dwell in

your neighborhood and to perceive the goings on in a world still chaotic in its ways.

"To have lived in an environment where goods, services, ideas and intellectual property were freely shared, it has been an eye-opener for me to visit a civilization where little is shared without it requiring payment of some kind. I have found a culture where patents are awarded for discoveries dealing with essential, survival commodities such as food and medicine, and where even common language needs to be trademarked and copyrighted.

"We witness your modes of operation, your ways of doing things, and in almost all instances you must chose the better of two or more options, and, or, often the lesser of two or more evils, to survive in this world. And it is the fear of non-survival, and the need to jealously protect self, by individuals and corporations alike that have set the tone for abundance for each to be siphoned off into the overflowing 'portfolios' of the few.

"These circumstances make it difficult to live an ideal life, yet against the rather ideal model that is my world, I point out the enormous advantages of yours. In almost all you do there are choices, decisions to be made about the best ways or the lesser evils, and these decisions build character and strength, which is much less likely to be invested in on more regulated spheres.

"Countless, countless are the universe creatures that feel for you when you lose. Vast is the number of Our Father's progeny that rejoice, and cheer you on when you win. Myriad are your siblings that envy you your status on this world, that so cultivates the leaders, the decision-makers, yes, the politicians for His ever-expanding universes.

"Your opportunities for progression, for learning, for the further development of character brings to my mind the expression 'fabulous.' Few worlds in the local system will allow an individual to gain such a major head start in the process of ascension as is available to you on your world.

"You might surely visualize the near ideal workings on the planet from which I hail. And still, there is every *reason for your citizens to fare well on your world, where one must so frequently weigh up the greater good, to find the nearest, although often-still blemished best way to go about any project.*

Be assured that in your rejoicing over a victory, and your despair about a failure, there are always the likes of me who will 'look over' your lives, your wins and losses and wish that for their career starts such a trying, learning time could have been had.

"Do stay with the battle. There are countless beings that are monitoring the progress, the dedication, and the sizeable results of your cooperative endeavors that will help bring your world into Love and Light.

Charmed to be here, and pleased to add my contribution to Andrea's recent lesson, this is Samuel. I send my love to all."[102]

Samuel lived on Panoptia, and has given some insight into what his life was like on that planet.

So, if you don't get enough variation in your mortal life, you will in all probability at some stage join the ranks of those spirit guides who go to darkened planets, to help the struggling mortals there. And, in a second-hand way, you get to understand all the challenges they experience. But it's not a problem we Earthlings face. In fact, I gather the experiences we do have here, with just one life, are so tough that we produce amazingly versatile spirit beings, who will go on to share their experience and insights across the universes. Of course, having just read that transcript of the earthbound spirit Mrs. Simons in the previous chapter, it's obvious some of us must be very frustrating students, before we reach any spiritual heights.

Before leaving this topic, I will briefly turn to the subject of children in spirit. As we have seen, children can be found in the astral planes, and can even be found attached to living mortals. But I do not think that is the general "fate" of children – far from it. Fascinating descriptions of how children are raised in spirit are included in "Life in the World

---

[102] The Better of Two Options –
http://www.1111angels.net/old_files/E_Archives/list234.htm received by George Barnard on February 29th, 2004.

Is Reincarnation an Illusion?

Unseen", in "The Life Elysian" and in "Spirit World and Spirit Life."[103] This last book is comprehensive and very uplifting. One is really left with the impression that they are amazingly well looked after, and instructed by wonderful carers. It is also clear that the children actually "grow up", much as they do here. They are only kept from their earth parents if the latter have not demonstrated the sort of love that is normal. So they do keep in touch with their real earth parents in most cases. Here is a fascinating extract from "Spirit World and Spirit Life":

> When, after many months of silence, Dee came to us, the veil between the two worlds seemed to grow transparent. At first it was enough to know that she lived,—lived with her own personality, only intensified and made more beautiful. Then we began to ask questions concerning that life and its unfoldment to her, and soon we wished to know of her occupations. One evening we asked if she could tell us of her work. The reply came quickly:
> "Can you believe that I am developing into a teacher?"
> 'We surely can', we replied; 'but will you tell us just how and what you are teaching?'
> "I am teaching little children at present, and love the work. I tell them stories that have a lesson in them."
> 'Something like kindergarten work?'
> "Yes; and I love it; for the children are so quick to learn, and so loving, too. I like to mother the little things, so that they may not miss too much the care and tenderness of the mother left on earth."
> 'Can you give us some idea of the way you teach them?' "I will try. Today it was in this way:
> "'Once upon a time', I told them, 'there was a beautiful fairy who took little children to a wonderful garden where they could play. Then the fairy told them of a new game.' And here I tell it to them, pretending to quote the fairy's words. And so I draw them into all sorts of little, new, educational thoughts, by clothing the thought in a story.
> "Sometimes I describe animals on earth, and they are much interested because they have never seen them

---

[103] *"Spirit World and Spirit Life"* by Charlotte Elizabeth Dresser published in 1922.

Progress in Spirit.

here.[104] *You would laugh to see me trying to represent lions and tigers. But I do not tell them they would harm little children, because evil is not known to them. No thought of cruelty must be allowed to enter their minds."*

This description of her work made us wish to hear more, and one evening she gave us the following:

"My children are always the dearest work that I have, and I hope that I shall never stop teaching them. Would you like to hear about to-day's lesson?

"I wished to tell them a story of activity in work; so I described the little things of earth, like the ants and bees and other busy little creatures. The children wanted to know what they were like and I tried to tell them. But I could not quite make them understand. Then I tried to make pictures of them, but as I am no artist, that was not much better. So I finally said that the ants crawl and the bees fly. Then immediately we had a crawling, flying crowd of children that completely overwhelmed their teacher, and she called a halt to the lesson and joined in the fun!"

Again, when we asked for a "kindergarten" story, she told us the following:

"To-day I called a tiny child to come to me, and when I had her in my arms, I placed my hand on her head and said to the other children: 'Now this, where my hand is, is a beautiful house that we are going to furnish, and you may tell me what we should put in it'. One said, 'There must be a big room full of love', opening her arms as if she would enclose the universe. Another declared that we must put in kind thoughts for other children who had no mothers here. Another said we could 'make a playroom in the house, and play games, and see pictures of all those queer animals on earth'. Another thought, 'We might have a little mother's room, where we could mother other little children as you mother us'. I said, 'Do you think the rooms in this beautiful house are all filled now?'

One replied, 'Wouldn't love fill all the others?'

---

[104] This suggests strongly that the planes where children grow up are in the Spirit Spheres, and not in the astral plane. These places are described in Chapter 16.

Is Reincarnation an Illusion?

> *'Pretty near it', I said, 'but how about truth and knowledge and growth?'*
> *'Why, each of these could have a room, too', they said. And the little child in my arms began to feel her head to find where all these rooms could be."*
>
> *We asked once if she did not have many children come to her who had been wrongly taught, or not at all and therefore had only false ideas and impressions. My pencil wrote:*
> *"Most of them leave their false impressions with their bodies. One of the children here was a child of criminal parents, and came over poisoned by wrong teaching; but the influence here was so good and so gentle that she soon outgrew the other impressions. I think she would have drifted into a criminal life if she had been left on earth; here, she is very dear and good."*
> *'If every child had been surrounded by right influences, what would have happened?'*
> *"Most of them would have been good, I think; and their influence over the actually bad would have held evil actions in check."*

Another book that I discovered after the initial publication is a volume from a set of five volumes received by an English pastor – Rev. George Vale Owen. His fifth volume entitled "The Outlands of Heaven"[105] contains some amazing examples of games spirit children play in Chapters 7 and 8. Another extract from "The Life Elysian"[106] gives some ideas about the homes these children have, and again stresses the efforts to encourage the growth of a questioning mind:

> *Methods of treatment had been skillfully drawn from the best vintages of experience: adaptations had been critically made with a view to naturally meeting every possible requirement. Strength with growth, intrinsic character with interest, sweetness of disposition with progressive determination, humility with competence, love with power, and reverence with success. All these had*

---

[105] *"The Outlands of Heaven"*, Volume 5 of *"The Life Beyond the Veil"*, which can be found here: https://new-birth.net/link15/
[106] *"The Life Elysian"* by Robert James Lees, first published in 1905 –page 96.

to be accomplished, and were adequately provided for, together with a systematic but careful extraction of every hereditary proneness to the ignoble and impure. The correction of these latter tendencies is one of the child features to which special and ever watchful care has to be directed.

The home comprises a surprising number of palatial buildings, each of which is placed at a good distance from its neighbour and located in a retreat perfectly adapted to the particular use of its department. Among them I saw the Nursery where pre-natal children are specially cared for; dormitories—all young children requiring a certain amount of sleep—a gymnasium, museum, theatre, laboratory and other places answering to every possible demand which may arise. But the most striking adaptations were to be found in the open air, where a system of landscape gardening had been adopted, which I can only describe as the interrogative. Everything, everywhere, appeared to be designed to prompt questions, and so effectively was this carried out that I fell into the trap myself, and was asking for information at every turn of my head.

The existence of such institutions in Paradise equipped with every possible educational appliance beyond the powers of an earthly mind to understand, will be regarded by many—especially such as have been taught to think that an instant after death the soul of an infant explosively acquires all knowledge—as miserably materialistic and blasphemously untrue. I should pass such conclusion of superstitious ignorance in the silence it merits, were it not for the obstacle it throws in the path of honest inquirers who refuse to pass any objection unnoticed.

If we try to grasp intelligently an idea of what it is we are aspiring to—perfection and nearness to God—and the almost infinite distance by which our present imperfections separate us from that goal, then cast our eyes backwards to measure the comparatively short way we have as yet travelled on the journey since the pilgrimage of evolution first began, I think there will be little difficulty in recognizing that these preparatory stages of Paradise are an absolutely necessary provision if we are to succeed.

One of the interesting things about communications from spirit about spirit children is that there are apparently no "old souls" among them. All children are just children, and have to grow and be taught, just like they do here. So, in spite of what we may say here about spiritually precocious children, there is no evidence of this being true. I personally believe that children that are judged as "old souls" are in fact those that are in tune with their spirit guidance. Following this notion, there is also absolutely no feedback from spirit that any adult who arrives in spirit, shows any spiritual growth beyond that which was achieved in their immediate past earth experience. In fact, as we all know, people on earth do not readily remember past lives, and if in fact they manage to do so, it is typically only a snippet of an event in a life. So too, when they arrive in spirit they do not suddenly recall these supposed dozens or hundreds of past Earth lives that so many people claim to have experienced. If they do not show any spiritual advantage from these, and cannot recall them in full detail, it's surely much more likely that they simply have not experienced any such multiple past earth lives?

In one channeled book, it is even claimed that those mortals arriving in spirit who neglected their spiritual side while on earth, have very small spirit bodies, even childlike. And that this does not change until they have completed some basic education. As I have only read on this in one source, I am unsure of its veracity.

So, if we do progress in spirit, then what is the benefit of returning to Earth? And, more to the point, since spiritual progress is part and parcel of eliminating Karmic debt, or if you prefer, sin, at some stage the spirit will discover it is perfect. What I mean is that spiritual progress and perfection go hand in hand. If Karma can only be worked out on Earth, then it should not be possible to progress in spirit. But it is. Not just as slowly as here, but much faster than here. And as we can see, even children grow and have fun.

Chapter 14

Hearing from famous spirits.

There is a serious fundamental problem with mediumship, in that the beliefs of the medium will intrude into what is received, even if the person both takes great care to try to limit this, and has some feedback on the process. So I am aware that even as I might accuse others of being confused about what they are receiving from spirit, so too can that accusation be leveled at the mediums that I might choose. It is for this reason that many folks have given up on channeled material. It is contradictory. Heck there is a popular book, which I will not give any further energy to by mentioning the author or title, which claims to have been the product of some materialized spirit beings, and these beings claim to know that Jesus and his apostles have all reincarnated many times. Yet in my favourite source, not only do we hear from many of the apostles and Jesus himself, but they go to some lengths to state that they have not reincarnated, and explain why it is physically impossible to do so. It's no wonder folks give up on channeled material.

It is also the case that the level of the spirit has great influence on what is communicated, because as far as I have been able to discern, spirits even in very high spheres in the next realm may still believe in reincarnation. While one can attract spirits higher than that, it's extremely hard to prove this is the case to someone else, and many mediums are not even able to ask the questions that might reveal how advanced their guides really are. That Law of Attraction really does bring you a compatible spirit guide, one that pretty much believes as you do, unless you demand the truth, and are truly open to being challenged. Even then, guides try not to upset their fragile mortal charges.

Nevertheless on a site[107] that I am associated with, we now have a very long list of famous and infamous spirits, probably approaching 1,000. Some religious, many more not, and all still apparently alive, long after their death. Of many different beliefs. None claims to have been

---

[107] https://new-birth.net/link16/

Is Reincarnation an Illusion?

reincarnated. These include the apostles, Jesus, many American Presidents, famous religious figures like Martin Luther and Martin Luther King, even some more recent folks like Jerry Falwell and Harvey Milk. Hearing from these folks is exactly what I would expect, if my premise is correct. So I think that even if my audience is very suspicious that these messages come from who they claim to be, nevertheless one would truly expect these to exist, if reincarnation is false.

And, interestingly on this site this time scale covers almost 100 years of mediumship, with quite a number of different mediums. So it's not just one individual medium.

I will give some indication of the scope that is covered. There are significant numbers of messages from two folks who claim to be the mother and father of humanity – the very first humans. They have quite a lot to say, and they certainly do not claim to have ever reincarnated. No time scale is given for when they walked the earth, but I suspect based on other sources it is probably a million years ago. Interestingly they do not call themselves Adam and Eve, and I think there is good reason for that, Adam and Eve came along a lot later, and were not the very first humans. That you can discover in another source that also claims to come from discarnates – The Urantia Book.

There are also messages from inhabitants of Atlantis and from Greenland when it was more habitable. Also ancient spirits from the East, who in spite of never having experienced a reincarnation, claim that they do not know what else to believe in.

Then we have folks from Old Testament times, Cain, Abel, Aaron, Moses, Jochebed, Abraham and Sarah, Elias, Lot, Jacob, King David, Saul, Micah, Confucius, Jeremiah, Solomon, Noah and even Buddha. Closer to the New Testament we have of course large numbers of communications from Jesus, Mary, Mary Magdalene, Judas, John the Baptist, most of the Apostles, Constantine, Augustus Caesar, Julius Caesar, and many others and then we move into more modern times.

Here we have a great selection, including interesting bits from Shakespeare about his life, many of the American founding fathers, many of the past American presidents, Francis Bacon, Immanuel Kant, Layfayette, Otto von Bismark, Napoleon, Thomas Paine, Robert

Hearing from famous spirits.

Ingersoll, Ulysses Grant, Queen Elizabeth I, Queen Victoria, Neville Chamberlain, Walt Disney, Emmett Till, Ida Tarbell and on and on. Literally almost thousands, certainly a very great number of interesting folks who have passed on. Some messages are too short to tell much, others are simply fascinating.

Is this proof? Of course not. But it's what you should expect to find if reincarnation is false, and communication across the veil is achievable.

Chapter 15

Indwelling Spirits – the perfect Guide.

If it is as I have suggested, and every one of us has a Divine guide whose job it is to guide us through all our free will choices, then what is the point of returning endlessly to the same stage – Earth. We have a guide that will lead us to perfection, and it becomes ever easier to hear this guidance as we progress through spirit, whereas it is extremely hard to actually discourse with this entity on Earth, although a small number of folks have achieved this. If we return endlessly to Earth, what happens to this guide? Does it have to put up with our slow progress? In fact, this Divine Guide is with us for a long time in spirit, but there is evidence that those who refuse the last step – the Seventh Sphere - subsequently lose their Indwelling Spirit. They then have no path to divinity, and the Indwelling Spirit gains a new mortal to shepherd through time and space, one that hopefully is more willing to travel the whole journey.

Incidentally, I might add a bit here from Sylvia's book. Sylvia Browne also describes the seven lower spheres, but her understanding of the seventh is somewhat off beam, in my opinion. She believes that spirits here give up their individuality and become absorbed into "God". In fact in some respects she is close – we understand these spirits do go through a transformation that results in their becoming something quite different. They do become "at-one" with God, but, as you could discover in the case of Judas, they still have their unique personality and individuality. Sylvia tells of the Seventh sphere:

> *Level Seven: The level to which only a few rare[108] souls choose to advance, where the spirit forfeits its identify and is willingly absorbed into the "uncreated mass," or the infinite, unfathomable force field from which the love and power of God emanate.[109]*

---

[108] That this is rare is desperately sad. But apparently true. The greater part of our eternal growth path lies beyond that Seventh sphere.
[109] *Life on The Other Side*, page 185.

Is Reincarnation an Illusion?

Francine goes on to tell of a short visit to the seventh:

> *Francine once had a very brief glimpse through the "veil," as she describes the boundaries between dimensions, into Level Seven. She could vaguely make out a few very indistinct physical forms, but she was so completely overwhelmed by the intensity of God's palpable presence that she quickly backed away from it.*[110]

The impression that Francine received is in fact acknowledged by James Padgett, where it is pointed out that only Divine Love spirits can live in the Seventh Sphere, and that Sixth Spherians simply would be very uncomfortable there. Indeed the Fifth Sphere is very similar, as that is also a Divine Love sphere. But this tale about what happens in the Seventh sphere is quite different to that expressed by James Padgett and the messages he received, the story in The Urantia Book, and indeed the few messages Judas has delivered on the subject.

But one can discern the source of Sylvia's concern, and one would sympathise, if the point were true. She is fearful that she will lose her individuality. Of more interest is the fact that Francine found the atmosphere in the seventh sphere quite distasteful, which is exactly in line with that channeled by James Padgett. This is what he delivered:

> *As you may know these Celestial Spheres are above the spiritual spheres, and are inhabited only by spirits who have received the New Birth and who believe in the Truths as taught by Jesus.* ***No other spirits are permitted to enter these spheres, and no other spirits could possibly find any happiness in them, for in them Divine Love is so developed in the souls of the spirits who live there that any spirit not having that Love would find that he is in an atmosphere that is entirely foreign to his qualifications, and he would be most unhappy.*** *But as I say, no spirit who has not that Divine Love, which we tell you about, can possibly enter into these spheres. The walls of demarcation are just as solid*

---

[110] *Life on The Other Side*, page 186.

Indwelling Spirits – the perfect guide.

and forbidding as are walls of demarcation in your prisons on Earth from the outside world.

I live in a city that is most wonderful in its beauty and magnificence, and is filled with structures that surpass anything that you possibly conceive of.

This city is inhabited by spirits who have a wonderful soul development, and are capable of understanding the deep truths of God, which are not given to mortals or spirits in the spiritual spheres.

This may seem a little strange to you, but it is true; for it would be utterly impossible for the spirits of these lower spheres, or for mortals, to understand these higher truths. They cannot be comprehended with what you call the intellectual faculties or the mind, but can be only understood by the soul's perceptions, developed to such a degree that nothing that partakes of the purely material can have an abiding place in that soul.

The mind must stop in its progress at the sixth sphere, and after that only the soul can progress. But this does not mean that the spirit who makes such progress in the Celestial Heavens does not increase in knowledge and understanding, for he does to a greater extent than it could be possible for the mere mind to progress; but this progress of a spirit in knowledge and understanding is a progress of the soul perceptions, of which I speak. The faculties of the soul are as far superior to and above the faculties of what you call the mind as are the heavens above the Earth.[111]

To summarise James Padgett's findings, there are two paths through spirit, a natural love path and a Divine (agape) Love path. The vast majority of spirits are currently following a natural love path, in spite of the efforts that Jesus put into teaching the Divine Love path. The natural love path includes all religions, and even those folk that are simply intellectual by nature, and Judge David Hatch would be a perfect example of that.

---

[111] John, the Apostle, describes the difference between the spirits of the Celestial and the Spirit Spheres and their happiness, https://new-birth.net/link17/ received by James Padgett on September 25th, 1915

Is Reincarnation an Illusion?

Now the lower Spirit Spheres are traversed by all spirits, but the Third, Fifth and Seventh are primarily Divine Love spheres, and the Seventh is exclusively a Divine Love Sphere. Those following this Divine Love path spend very little time in the Sixth, as they find that sphere distasteful, and they remain in the Fifth until they can traverse to the Seventh. A natural love spirit, resident in the Sixth, who decided that he would like to follow the Divine Love path, will need to return to the Third, to as it were, develop his Divine Love training wheels.

Once a spirit has completed the Seventh, he or she is ready to fuse with their Indwelling Spirit. This will create a new eternal being, with the personality and memories of the mortal, and the intellect and memories and divinity of the Indwelling Spirit. This entity is "one with God", and will always seek to do His Will. Does this being have free will? Apparently yes. The next question that I asked was whether it is possible for this being to err, or sin. And the answer is that it can will that. But, since an Indwelling Spirit has never gone astray, I wonder how a fused mortal can go astray. I would guess the chances are extremely unlikely. Since following the Will of God always leads to happiness, there is no reason other than pride to seek any other path.

This discussion of the availability of a perfect Divine Guide concludes my discussion of reincarnation. If the information I have shared is true, it certainly makes little sense to return to Earth, to a place where we have great difficulty hearing our guide. The Urantia Book makes it quite clear that those who choose to ignore the leadings and promptings of this Guide, will lose that Guide.

I think that it may be fair for me at this stage to summarise what I believe happens "on the other side." We will do this in the final chapter.

Chapter 16

What really happens after death?

Death.

I guess the first question to ask is whether we all survive death? Until recently I would not have had any doubt about that, but it seems there is a small complication for some people. Many people would be aware that the universe appears to attempt to supply that which we focus on, even if it is not good for us. Those people who are adamant that there is no life after death, and make this a certainty in their life often do not pass immediately from one realm to the next in a conscious state. They are termed "sleeping survivors."[112] These folks almost get their most fervent wish - annihilation. They may sleep for centuries, before a group awakening. More recent information now suggests that relatively few pass over as "Sleeping Survivors" at the present time. (See Chapter 9) This may be because the rules have been changed, as we enter the "Correcting Time" and also possibly because there are far more Celestial helpers available at this time. I assume these "tough cases" were grouped together as an efficiency measure which enabled them to handle these folks en-mass.[113]

But the majority of us simply pass from one state to another, with very little lost time. Some reports state three days are lost in this transition, but I now believe that is almost certainly incorrect, and may simply be an attempt to use some Biblical material, since the N.T. talks about Jesus being resurrected after three days. Depending on your physical health as you depart this life, you may be instantly conscious of your existence in the next realm, or require some healing in the next. Thus you may pass almost without any break in consciousness. Obviously one would not be aware of lost time, so this issue is impossible to

---

[112] The Urantia Book mentions these on page 340.
[113] A wonderful example is contained in Letter 38 in *"Letters from the Light"* published by Beyond Words Publishing and based on the out of print publication *"Letters from a living dead man"* where it is Letter 39.

answer accurately without third party feedback. However there are many stories which suggest almost no break in "time" occurs.

If you are awake, there is no knowing quite how death will unfold. This is because as the brain shuts down, you can experience many different effects. Most of these are anything but spiritual, although you might think that they do feel spiritual. They are simply the results of the brain shutting down. You might have a "life review", sort of like a movie. You may see white tunnels, or black tunnels. You might even have an instant out of body experience, where you are floating above your body, looking down on the scene, and that certainly is a spiritual event. Sometimes if the physical body is about to be badly damaged, the spirit body is withdrawn before impact or injury. This gives rise to the out of body experience, where you look down as an outsider on your own body, and will avoid you feeling any pain.

If you are consciously expecting death, things are probably going to be a bit different. Many people know that they are dying, and seem to gain additional abilities or insights in the last hours or days. They often start to see their spirit guides, and may feel the presence of their love, and be quite calm. There is no reason to panic. For one it is not going to help, and secondly, for the vast majority of us, what follows is a big improvement over life on earth. The spirit folks who are full time workers assisting us to pass over will be in attendance at your passing. Generally this job is left entirely to these skilled beings, and your spirit family generally waits until you are settled, and then arrives to welcome you. If you are weakening in the last hours of life, you most likely may see one or two of these spirit beings who assist, as this will limit any concern when you see them from the other side.

You might be met by dear loved ones who passed over before you, but it is more likely it will be one of those tasked with this function. As you pass through death, initially they may be seen only as a bright white light. This is the basis of the reported white tunnel. Some folks have reported meeting Jesus, (if Christian!) but this is very unlikely to happen. Not that he is not around, but if he was there, you almost certainly would not recognize him – unless you already know what he looks like – and more to the point he has far more important things to be doing. Might he have welcomed Mother Teresa? I think that is very likely, but I do not know that for a fact, but I do know of another individual he did welcome. Take it from me, you need to have been doing a pretty special job on earth to warrant that compliment. And the chances are that you would not need to be reading this book, if that is true. But the folks who assist with this transition know what they are doing, and some of them could appear like a very advanced spirit being. But generally they try to appear as non-threatening as possible and adjust their clothing to suit the occasion.

However it seems that those who see the "tunnel of light" or actually recognize some of the beings, who are there to meet the newly departed, are in the minority. Far too many depart this life with inadequate spiritual preparation, and the result is that they have great difficulty in triggering their spiritual vision and spiritual hearing. You can imagine that moving from a situation where you operate out of a physical brain, even though it is linked to a spirit mind, is a very different situation when that physical brain is gone, and you must operate entirely with spirit faculties. The result is that many spend a period of time in a dazed state, in almost complete silence, and in almost total darkness. In the meantime, their "greeters" are frantically trying to make some sort of break through. So if it happens to you, and you hear music, or see shadows or faint voices, do make an effort to hear and see more clearly. The irony is that because the next realm is subject to the influence of our thoughts, simply believing and saying: "I can see" or "I can hear" will trigger the required spiritual vision and hearing.

You may notice that you are completely naked, but this is not often the case. Probably because almost immediately, your spirit companions will "create" spirit clothes for you. There are various opinions as to whether they wear diaphanous gowns, or clothes that you are familiar with. It seems that it varies, and varies particularly according to your station in the next realm. So the attendants may in fact change into our style of clothing for some hours to ease the transition and avoid scaring you. These spirit clothes are great. They don't get dirty and they don't wear out either. And you can change them just by thinking up a new outfit, assuming you are sufficiently spiritually advanced. But as individuals progress, they seem to all adopt a sort of diaphanous gown which has very specific colours reflecting the development and even the personality of the individual.

The very first thing that is going to happen to you, as you begin to realize something strange is happening, is that you will travel. I have only a vague idea how far that is, and it will probably not take more than a few seconds, or maybe a few minutes. While a lot of people report going to a way station, each person can have a unique experience. So from this point on, it's very hard to say what will exactly happen to you. For example if you departed this earth life in need of significant spiritual repair, it's almost certain you will be taken unconscious to a hospital (albeit rather different to ours!) for recovery, and you would regain your consciousness in that location. This repair can cover emotional as well as physical weaknesses. Some people are in effect scarred by their life experiences and need considerable work before they are freed from these effects. Curiously the material and the physical worlds can be quite interwoven, to have outcomes in the spiritual realm that result from the physical.

Let's assume that you will arrive at a way station, a collection point for recently deceased individuals, as this is relatively common. No doubt with much coming and going. It is very pleasant, attractive, with a very loving atmosphere, and you will soon feel very relaxed. It has been described as a station concourse, but I don't think that describes a loving atmosphere, although it may well be accurate in terms of comings and goings, and meeting loved ones. Sometimes these places are described as outside, on a hillside. It will undoubtedly feel like the best place you have ever been to. Things are looking up, you conclude. When you arrive in the next realm you will immediately notice an up step in frequency, not just in your own spirit body but in your surroundings as well. What you begin to experience is a higher frequency in which you exist. The colours are more vibrant; the plant life is more lush and alive.

If at this point you start to think about what you have left behind, you might find that you are right back there. In other words, you can travel, virtually instantly, just by thinking about it. So you might well see your family back on earth shedding tears about your passing. But they won't see you, or hear you. You are much better off at this stage going back to the transition place; particularly as at this very early stage you will still have strong earth attractions. Later on it is safer to travel back to earth because these ties will have dissipated. Back on "earth" you may be able to see everything just as you used to, but you will find that nothing is solid. You can pass through people, walls, everything. But the ability to discern things on earth seems to be inversely related to the degree of spiritual advancement of the

What really happens after death?

individual, and is one of the faculties that can be lost quite quickly. So some people can see the earth and its human forms relatively clearly in this early stage if they are somewhat unevolved spiritually, while others have as much difficulty as we do in seeing spirit. However, you will notice that you can "hear" dear mortal friends thinking about you, and you may almost instantly visit them. If you are really lucky, you may find a few who can "feel" your presence, and this will give you a big thrill, just as it will give them a thrill to know you are around. You may even be able to create a few "signs" that let folk know you are still around. Things like leaving a telltale cigar smell, or making a noise or two, or leaving your favourite flower where it will be seen, or perhaps by leaving a scent in the air. How they do those things? Frankly I didn't know until I read Chapter 13 of "More Alive Than Ever", ...Always Karen..[114]

But back at the way-station, things are very solid. You can hug old friends, and they can certainly "hear" you. The spirit body appears very solid, and still appears to need to breathe, but does not need sleep or food as sustenance. But in the early phase sleep may be required; however that phase will soon pass. While you can talk in the old conventional way, you will also discover that it seems to be possible to converse just via thoughts. Then you notice that they must be hearing your thoughts, and you hearing their thoughts. And then you have a dreadful realization – these folk know everything about you! They can simply read your memories. And they hear your thoughts! You recall that time you got Fred fired by making up a confidential report, and rather stretching the facts to suit, now here you have to look Fred in the eye. He knows, but strangely he's not mad. Or maybe, you remember wearing that really low cut dress for the Christmas party and how successful it was in starting that affair with Joe. And here is Sally, Joe's partner, smiling at you. Total openness leads to the rapid realization that all of us fail from time to time. Actually not all thoughts are shared, so we can still have some secrets! And only those more advanced can actually read the history of a spirit in its mind storage.

During this period of orientation, you start to notice that not all spirits are quite the same. Some have a beautiful countenance and way about them. And they are brighter, and amazingly loving. This brightness

---

[114] This book can be found at https://new-birth.net/link8/

seems to come right out of them. Others are baser, dark, indeed some are downright ugly. As you wonder why this might be, you suddenly begin to wonder where you fit in. Are you ugly, or beautiful? Bright or dark?

At this point you will also know that you are just the same person that you were in the mortal life. With the same beliefs, memories, attitudes, values, fears, unresolved issues and loves. How did this happen? After all, your brain is already consigned to dust. Quite simply as a mortal on earth you had three major components. There was your soul, which as far as we can tell, was probably billions of years old. Then there was your spirit body, which encapsulates the soul, and takes on the appearance of the mortal body. Just as well, because none of us can see souls, but we can see spirit bodies. It seems that the spirit body is a sort of reflection of the enclosed soul. If this soul is pure, the spirit body is literally full of light. If the soul is tarnished, the spirit body is dark, even ugly. And finally of course you had a mortal body. While you may have thought that all your memories were in your brain, it seems it is not quite so. The spirit body houses the mind, and the brain is the transducer that allows the physical body to interact with the spirit body and its mind. So you may have lost the physical body, but most folks report feeling much lighter, and far prefer only having a spirit body. For one thing, it has no defects. If you lost a leg, you will find you are now perfect. If your brain suffered from senile dementia, you will have no such limitation now. And there are some neat tricks you will learn in the future in regards to your spirit body as you progress spiritually. I have recently learnt that the spirit body itself is complex, and has at least two constituents, one being a relatively gross astral body, and the other a more etheric spirit body.

Just at this point, the spirits who manage this transition process explain that in the heavens the Law of Attraction is paramount. Every spirit has to live where it fits in – where it is in harmony. And, yes, those beautiful ones, that seem somehow ethereal, are more advanced, and no, most probably you won't live with them. You can look down at your hands, or ask for a "mirror" to see how you rate. They will explain that you can progress beyond where you start out, but probably you won't be listening closely enough. You may be concerned that you are not going to be living with your dear Madge who passed some years before you. She says that she will come and visit you regularly. Things are rapidly beginning to sound more complicated.

Is Reincarnation an Illusion?

The Structure of the Heavens.

I guess many practical folk have long realized you can get almost no sense out of most religions when you ask about heaven. All that singing and harp plucking stuff that is supposed to go on, and strutting around on streets of gold. Or maybe the idea that you are going to be asleep until some great day of judgment. And particularly the notion that you will be magically, and instantly "perfect".

It is far more logical to consider that since mortals have been around a very long time, probably over a million years on earth, that there has been a heaven all that time, with spirits in it. Certainly the holy books, like the Bible, happily report interactions with the spirit world going back many years before Jesus. Perhaps I should point out here, that the spirit realm that I am about to discuss would appear not to be the **Kingdom of God** that so many orthodox Christians expect to enter via Jesus' help. This is undoubtedly the cause of a great deal of confusion, and even heartache. It is what has led so many Christians to conclude, incorrectly, that only they will get to "heaven" and everyone else will only get to "hell." The real issue is "which" heaven, something they have not considered, even though a significant clue is given in the Bible that there may be more than one "heaven", in a reference to the "third heaven" in the New Testament.[115] The main part of this paper covers the **Kingdom of Spirit**, also called the Spirit Spheres and not the **Kingdom of God**.

It may even be the case that we create this spirit heaven ourselves. Not to suggest God has nothing to do with it, but as spirits we have great powers, which powers increase as the spirit advances. So it would not surprise me if in fact the "realities" that are found are created by the spirits that are there. And this creation need not necessarily be conscious. This would explain why some spirits, and indeed many NDE's, (Near Death Experiences) seem to describe confusingly different places. We have explanations of Jewish heavens, and the classic Christian heavens, complete with harps, witnessing and bright holy images. We have descriptions of fire and brimstone

---

[115] **2 Corinthians 12:2**: I know a man in Christ who fourteen years ago was caught up to the third heaven. Whether it was in the body or out of the body I do not know—God knows.

What really happens after death?

hells, and also dark places that are simply cold, sad, dead places. One thing that is quite clear, the belief system of the spirit has a very large effect on the experience it will have. Whether this is only a function of the Law of Attraction, which causes like-minded spirits to congregate, or whether it is the will of the spirit that creates a "reality" it expects, is uncertain. But what is certain, is that real places exist that vary substantially.

The most common description of the Kingdom of Spirit talks about seven "spheres" or "worlds". However these should not be taken too literally. But it seems that however they are constructed, they are immense in size. There is absolutely no shortage of space.

Then there are also the vast uncountable heavens beyond the Seventh Sphere. Where are all these places? Well, we are not sure, but the universe is very much larger than man has supposed. Apparently what we humans think is the entire universe is but a very tiny corner of one of many super universes.[116] And some 80% of the material is apparently not visible to man anyway, but is visible to spirit. Could it be another dimension? It almost certainly is, because the First Spirit Sphere is located right here, somewhere in the space created by our orbit round the sun. That is extremely large, and obviously very close. But irrespective of the number of time/space dimensions that may exist, the distances involved in traversing our Universe are immense. Added to this, the solid material of the next realm can co-exist in space with solid material from our realm. So different solid objects can occupy the same spot, one in each dimension.

One of the difficulties or problems in getting a good description of the heavens comes from the apparent fact that the bottom up view is so limited and confused. Folks enter at the bottom of this schema, with very limited knowledge, and so they have to learn a great deal, over many years, before they could really be considered to know. And even then, as we will see later, time in spirit does not equate to advancement.

We are accustomed, on earth, to always know who is in charge, and how things are organized. But in the next realm free will is paramount. You will not be used to this idea, as earth is quite

---

[116] The Urantia Book

Is Reincarnation an Illusion?

different. If you want to believe something, you will be allowed to believe that, and furthermore, the Law of Attraction will ensure that you find yourself amongst others of like mind, who will agree with your outlook. So, you will be in the situation that unless you ask for information, you will be left with your belief. It is not going to happen that someone will knock at your door, proselytize and hand out a few pamphlets. That might be a relief for quite a few of us! Even the issue of religious groups is interesting. There are still many folks in spirit that insist on following their old earth based religion. However they are absolutely not allowed to proselytize.

There is another problem. Spirits are confined, to a large degree, to the sphere in which they reside. This is where they are in harmony, and they would not feel comfortable any higher or lower in the scheme. This does not mean that all in the same sphere are identical in outlook. One can still find intellectuals and religious folk in the same sphere, but typically not in close proximity. Indeed there are many such diverse groupings, called planes, within each sphere.

There is also the issue that your perception is a function of your spiritual development. So, if you are in the First sphere, you may be told there are other spheres, but you may not be able to see them. This is not like living in Australia, and knowing that there are other continents, such as the Americas, and knowing you could live there if you wanted to, or go there for an extended holiday. It is possible to have a very short visit to a higher sphere, but to achieve this you need to be taken there by someone with the spiritual power to enable you to travel there. What I am sure of is that you will find Catholics living together, groups of intellectuals, Muslims, Jews, Buddhists etc. And each of these groups will believe that their current happiness is a function of what they believe. This is not surprising, except if they compared themselves carefully with others, this would immediately illustrate the falsity of the idea. In this sense I describe things as confused from the bottom up.

A great many other folks have simply given up their earth based religious beliefs. In fact in the list of sources are a few books by Monsignor Robert Hugh Benson (received by Antony Borgia[117]) who although a Roman Catholic cleric, gave up all his prior religious beliefs

---

[117] *"Life in the World Unseen"*, by Anthony Borgia

inside a few hours. Such is the reality of the next realm that many of peoples' earth beliefs simply cannot withstand the reality. And I suspect that the rest who cling to outdated beliefs, as though it is a sort of security blanket, simply because it is what they are used to. And in yet others, it is because they don't know what else to believe. Indeed modern statistics will tell us only a small percentage of us are "early adopters" – people who are happy to try new things and are actively out there looking for new experiences.

There is no overall agreement about what happens next, and what is best for spiritual progression or what is the "right" belief. In fact I don't even think these lower spirits generally know who is in charge, and maybe some are only vaguely aware of the desirability of seeking to progress. So I would guess there may be spirits in the First Sphere who might dispute that there is a Second Sphere, never mind an almost unlimited number beyond that!

Those "in charge" always respect the free will choices of these spirits, so it is only through a conscious choice to follow a leader's direction, that people can be said to be led. The leaders are far more advanced, live somewhere else where you cannot go, and cannot be seen unless they decide to make themselves visible. This is because the more advanced spirits have an ability to conceal themselves from less advanced spirits. In some ways it is like it is on earth when we try to understand what happens after death. Our perception of the next realm is limited, and indeed there are many on earth that would dispute that there is any life after death.

The authority that we were used to on earth is simply absent. In that sense you can experience total freedom of choice to do as you please. Whether that might be doing something, or doing almost nothing. But it also means you can follow dozens of spiritual paths that don't lead anywhere special. In fact almost everything that you do will probably lead to increased happiness, so it is very easy to believe you are on the "right" path. And this is typically how spirits continue. They ascribe their current happiness to the path they are on, but it may be that there is nothing special about that path compared to many other paths.

However in another respect the spheres are supremely organized, with no chaos or poor organization. There is always someone in

Is Reincarnation an Illusion?

charge of a specific function, and they love their job, and have been superbly trained to perform it perfectly. So if you feel like being trained in a specific activity, this can be accomplished perfectly.

Of course there are other things that make it easy. You don't need to eat, although folks apparently enjoy nuts and fruits in the Spirit Spheres. They don't have digestive organs, so these foods are not eaten as we do on earth, but apparently more like "inhaled." The same with water, this refreshes, but is not used to sustain. Since you don't need to eat, clearly you don't need a job to earn money to survive. Indeed there is no money, because all you need is given. So, you will do things because you enjoy them, not because you have to. Well, that depends on where you are. These comments would appear to not apply in the lowest planes of the First Sphere that we will talk about soon.

Although we describe the Spirit Heavens as having seven spheres, in reality there are an almost infinite number of "planes" within these. In a sense, one's spirituality acts like a sort of gravity. The less spiritual you are, the further down you will sink, possibly right to the bottom. And the bottom is called hell. In fact, the really advanced spirits consider that all of the First and Second Spheres contain some darkness. But, for us earthlings, anything from the top of the First Sphere upwards is just great. There are in fact three portions of the First Sphere that could almost be called separate spheres, and seem to be numbered separately by Spiritualists. They typically also name them such as Twilight Lands, Dawn Lands and Summerland. But before we talk about these dark places, we will discuss the Astral Plane.

The Astral Plane.

The Astral Plane is a grosser dimension than the Spirit Spheres, and is a physicality just as the Spirit Spheres are. Very little has been received about this plane, and that is yet another reason why some reports about life after death appear to contradict each other – the Spiritual Laws here are different to those in the Spirit Spheres. Some spirits seem not to know that they are in the Astral Plane, and this is the home of earth bound entities. The term "earth bound" is given by spiritualists to spirits that are here around the earth, and they often try to convince them to "pass over".

There are higher levels and lower levels of the Astral Plane, and it exists both above and below the surface of the Earth. The Earth Plane is the third of the seven divisions of the Astral Plane. However, in order to reach the Spirit Spheres proper, we have to discard both our physical bodies, and another body called an astral body. People who have out of body experiences can travel in the astral, using their astral body, or leave the astral body and the physical body, and travel in the spirit spheres with their spirit body. It seems the silver chord that is reported as joining us to our physical bodies while alive is a part of the astral body, so any reports of entities with silver chords indicates they are astral travelling. Some references to the Astral Plane simply use the word "Earth Plane" as the description, probably because the Astral Plane is in very close proximity to earth. In any event, one of the seven planes in the Astral is itself called the Earth Plane.

Although earlier I described the "passing over" after death to a special arrivals area for newly arrived spirits, there have been countless descriptions of others who did not even notice that they had died, so instantaneous was their transition. These folk, sometimes even thirty years after death still do not realize that they are dead. Very frequently their description is of passing from life to death virtually instantly, only that the room and mortals that were there pre-death suddenly become hard or impossible to see clearly. These events seem typical of passing to the Astral Plane, rather than the Spirit Spheres. Another difference, related to the Astral Plane, is spirits reporting that immediately after death that they are tied to something, which may last hours or days, although time is hard to discern, but during that period they may notice the funeral and burial. It appears that the astral body may take quite some time to separate from the physical body after death, and this gives the sensation of being tied to an invisible object. It is the silver chord which ties the astral body to the physical body which has not yet broken.

While I cannot be sure that the arrivals areas described earlier are all located in the Spirit Spheres, I currently believe that to be the case. The spirit can however only reach an arrivals hall if the recently deceased mortal is not still wearing their astral body. The older one is, the more likely that one's astral body will decay rapidly after death and release one for the Spirit Spheres. The same is true of those that are advanced spiritually. But those that die young have a very strong astral body, and they will often spend considerable time in the astral planes, of which there are seven, until they are able to cast off the astral body. The astral plane appears to give spirits who had very little earth time an opportunity to find their way spiritually. They can interact with both evil ex-mortals and spiritually advanced ex-mortals here, and they have an added ability that deception is not possible on this plane. However if they are attracted to earthly pleasures, this desire will remain, and can prove their undoing. It also seems to be the case that accidental death may result in the spirit arriving in the Astral Plane. This seems to happen to soldiers in wartime, as an example. But it may be as much to do with their relative youth.

Those that fall into this category without exception have no understanding of what really happens after death. Many believe that the dead lie asleep until the "great resurrection." With that in mind, they conclude they can't be dead. Others don't even have that concept and just complain that they can no longer see because of the darkness. But later they recover their vision, and find a world that is very similar to earth, yet with differences.

Other spirits of a very material bent find themselves in the Earth plane. There seem to be many reasons for this. They may have had an unexpected bad experience, such as being murdered, and this may have left them with a desire for revenge. It seems the shock of a sudden death may indeed be a factor in how successfully one transitions. They may also be of limited spiritual development, but not necessarily bad. Another reason is a desire to look after a family, or even to try to enjoy, or protect material possessions. They may then hang around their last place of living for a long period of time. Some

What really happens after death?

are intensely religious, but of the mindless type. Yet they start out no better off than someone who never gave life after death a moment's thought.

In the Astral Plane, it is possible to eat and drink, and apparently the astral body will produce excreta. However there is no need for either and this is typical of the choices spirits face. If they indulge the desire for food and drink, this generally leads to a dark entity suggesting at some time that they can get a better experience by obsessing a living mortal. And since that carries a heavy spiritual penalty, eventually they pass into the hells. There are churches here too, but sadly they seem incapable of actually teaching anything more useful than that learned on earth, and many of the pastors are here precisely because they are not spiritual.

There is also a class of entity which we often see as "ghosts", who are not actually earth bound spirits. Specifically in the case where a mortal has a lot of negative experiences, as might be if they were tortured, murdered, or otherwise badly treated, these experiences have to be resolved. And until they are resolved, which includes the individuals who caused the trauma, they may leave an energetic signature which behaves and looks like an earthbound. In fact these are simply astral shells, devoid of a soul, because the individual has moved into the spirit spheres, but this energetic bundle still may be tied to a location or another entity in darkness. It is very difficult from our side of the veil to know whether one is dealing with an astral shell sans soul, or a real spirit entity. These astral shells are dissipated only when the emotional issues surrounding them are resolved. There are some other entities in the Astral Plane, some of which are wonderful, and others which are dangerous. Provided that you have not distanced yourself from your guide you will be protected, but if you have totally ignored spiritual matters your guide will not be there to protect you, and the experience can be very unpleasant. While a spirit body can experience pain, and even be apparently damaged, it repairs itself rapidly, but it cannot be destroyed. The astral body will also repair itself normally, but as it is not eternal in nature, apparently it can be completely destroyed by some of the evil elementals, and this results in that (dark) spirit passing into the dark planes of the First Sphere – hell. This sort of thing can only happen in the lowest of the astral divisions, which are considered the anti-chamber of hell.

Is Reincarnation an Illusion?

Hell.

Let's start by pointing out that the classic description of hell given by churches is very inaccurate. Fire and brimstone is not how things are. You will also find plenty of "new age" folk will deny there is any hell at all, no matter how it is constructed. They will tell you they have never had any feedback from the other side to suggest anything like it. They report that all spirits are loving and that there is only love. That may be so mostly because very few spirits in hell are keen to admit this to loved ones on earth. It is also the case that folks who are able to astral travel have reported that they cannot find a hell. That would be correct since the Astral Plane does not contain hell. This is a part of the Spirit Spheres and is not reachable if you are travelling in the astral.

Certainly there are not a great number of detailed reports[118] of life in the darkest spheres, but there are enough to satisfy a determined researcher. I have personally worked with people who were seriously troubled by dark spirits, and my mother has also told me my sister is (or was) in darkness. And, once you understand how the universe works, there has to be a place where those who are seriously out of harmony reside until they learn. It is just inconceivable that God would suddenly make loving spirits out of those who have chosen to be unloving. No, our progress is entirely dependent upon ourselves. That is what it means to be a free will creature. We must create ourselves and the result is our responsibility.

What is it like in hell? Here is a description:

> *In this hell of mine, and there are many like it, instead of beautiful homes, as the other spirits described, we have dirty, rotten hovels all crooked and decayed, with all the foul smells of a charnel house ten times intensified, and instead of beautiful lawns and green*

---

[118] James Padgett did receive a very great number of communications from folks in the hells, but I would not call these particularly detailed descriptions, although some are relatively detailed. Many of these can be found on the web here: https://new-birth.net/link19/
I have only found two books with an extensive treatment of the dark planes. These are *"A Wanderer in the Spirit Lands"* by Franchezzo and *"Gone West"* by J.S.M Ward.

meadows and leafy woods filled with musical birds making the echoes ring with their songs, we have barren wastes, and holes of darkness and gloom and the cries and cursings of spirits of damnation without hope; and instead of living, silvery waters we have stagnant pools filled with all kinds of repulsive reptiles and vermin, and smells of inexpressible, nauseating stinks.

I tell you that these are all real, and not creatures of the imagination or the outflowing of bitter recollections. And as for love, it has never shown its humanizing face in all the years that I have been here - only cursings and hatred and bitter scathings and imprecations, and grinning spirits with their witchlike cacklings. No rest, no hope, no kind words or ministering hand to wipe away the scalding tears which so often flow in mighty volumes. No, hell is real and hell is here.

We do not have any fire and brimstone, or grinning devils with pitch forks and hoofs and horns as the churches teach; but what is the need or necessity for such accompaniments? They would not add to the horrors or to our torments. I tell you my friend that I have faintly described our homes in these infernal regions and I cannot picture them as they are.

But the horror and pity of it all is that hope does not come to us with one faint smile to encourage us that there may at some time be an ending to all these torments, and in our hopeless despair we realize that our doom is fixed for all eternity.[119] (See a later explanation about the duration of hell.)

This is of course but one description, and as mentioned earlier, you should not be surprised to discover many variations on a theme. Some hells are places of isolation; others are cities of shared horrors presided over by tyrannical rulers with very nasty temperaments and stronger wills than their subjects.

Perhaps we should not use the word hell, because it is not a permanent situation, although commonly believed to be so by its inhabitants. There is no eternal damnation. In fact there is no

---

[119] https://new-birth.net/link10/ received by James Padgett, January 5th, 1916.

Is Reincarnation an Illusion?

damnation at all. Hell is simply a place where dreadful spirits live until they choose not to be dreadful. So how long could you be there then? It all depends on you. How low in the hells you are, and how soon you start to try to get out. Yes but how long? From feedback, there are two ways out, the normal way, which is pretty slow, and the short cut way.

The normal way involves the spirit realizing that he/she is there because of their attitudes and values, and then deciding to change, and slowly changing, by being kind to his companions. If you were really bad on earth you could expect this process to take longer than a lifetime, but it is often long because it may take the individual a very long time to discover that they are causing this unpleasant experience by virtue of their own behaviours. There is another curious thing about the hells that spirits trying to change seem to be more at the mercy of their compatriots than those who are not interested in change. The hells also seem to have well demarcated districts which are physically hard to exit; both in terms of finding a way out, and in getting past those that would prevent your exit. Generally it is only with the assistance of a substantially more developed spirit companion who is tasked with this job that anyone gets out.

Some historically bad spirits, like the Roman Emperors, seem to have spent up to a thousand years in darkness. Julius Caesar was still in hell in 1915, but got out with some help, in 17 months.[120] That means he had been in hell for 2040 years, a very long time indeed. Judas also learnt of the short cut, naturally from the apostles. Apparently Andrew and Mary Magdalene were always close to Judas, and they encouraged him to apply the knowledge that Jesus had taught them. Judas had not really understood these spiritual teachings, and in fact neither did the Apostles till after Jesus had departed. A more recent example is Neville Chamberlain,[121] whose appeasement policies effectively aided the Nazi regime, and is still paying the price, although he died in 1940.

The first thought that probably you might have, if you end up here, is that you did not appear to have a big day of judgment. You did not end up in front of God, and get judged. In fact, judgment happened every day and every second of your mortal life. When you broke a Spiritual

---

[120] https://new-birth.net/link20/ received by James Padgett May 1st 1917.
[121] https://new-birth.net/link21/ received by the medium FAB January 1st, 2011.

What really happens after death?

Law, your soul was encrusted immediately, and that was that. Now you have to in effect clean your soul yourself. You could have done that on earth, if you had chosen to, but it did not seem to affect your material life having an encrusted soul. Well I might debate how much real happiness and peace you felt on earth with a heavily encrusted soul, but you can retort that it did not affect starting the Ferrari. Or distributing illicit drugs, whatever took your fancy.

So how bad is hell really? It depends. Frankly, the upper reaches of "hell" would be better than many folk's experience of life on earth. The darkest depths are not good however. Here it is reported one can be in total darkness, unable to perceive anyone or anything, totally alone with only your own thoughts and memories. Many spirits report that they would choose annihilation, if it were an option. The emotional darkness and irritations and attentions of the other dark spirits make it a very unpleasant experience. It also appears that in the lowest of levels the spirit bodies are very dense and deformed. They appear to be affected by things like thirst and fire, even though these things do not affect more advanced spirits. It also appears possible to inflict physical damage on a spirit body, at the lowest levels, so that they do suffer injury and pain. And because the spirit body repairs itself very quickly, this pain can be repeated over and over again. The ability to move above the surface seems absent because these dark spirits are so gross. So they can be trapped in physical obstacles like swamps or holes, or have to physically ascend cliffs and mountains while trying to get out of some divisions.

What are my chances of ending up there? If you are a normal person, neither particularly good, nor particularly bad, then you will probably land up at the top of the first sphere. It could be a bit lower, or possibly a bit higher. You might not ever realize that this is "hell", and just think life after death is simply nowhere near what you had expected. On the other hand, if you were a poor African, or Asian, eking out a tough existence on earth, battling disease and hunger, trying to keep your children safe and alive, you may think this "hell" is a huge improvement over your earth experiences. If you have really tried on earth, and consider that you adhered strictly to your religious beliefs, and more particularly those relating to living in love, and caring for your fellows, which basically all religions espouse, you might make the Second Sphere, or higher. But statistically, the "normal" result is the first sphere.

Is Reincarnation an Illusion?

So how do you get out of darkness? Actually help is always available, although right at the bottom, it may take some time before that help can be perceived. The problem is that most spirits in darkness are too embarrassed to even acknowledge the help offered to them. We are none of us an island, and thus everyone knows someone, and so it's almost always the case that there is someone who you know, who is more advanced, and who you could therefore trust. The more advanced spirits are always trying to help those that are less developed, even in darkness, particularly if there is a personal relationship. But their advances are most often rebuffed. So the first lesson is to be prepared to ask for and accept help. The spirits that can help are those that are visually bright, or brighter than your companions. They will be loving too, which is always a clear indication.

The second lesson is to know that there is hope, and that hell is not eternal. The Christian Churches have done mortal man a great disservice in preaching that hell is eternal. Spirits either believe this themselves, or hear it constantly from their companions. Thus it is very hard to have hope. Admittedly the environment is not conducive to hope. Imagine this:

> *It seemed as if I was standing at the top of a mountain or hill. Below I could see a pretty valley, with forests, meadows, springs and streams. I heard birds singing, it was like a beautiful summer day. Suddenly, everything began to dry off. The green colors turned brown, the leaves fell off the trees, and after a short time, I saw a disastrous landscape. Everything was dry, the earth cracked, a few trunks like skeletons without life, the streams had disappeared, leaving behind only their stony beds. There was no sunshine anymore, everything seemed dark, like a winter dawn in the northern regions, but without snow, and the silence of death reigned.*[122]

Let's assume you accept help. There are two types of advice that you will get. The first is basically to develop your Natural love, and to start

---

[122] https://new-birth.net/link11/ received by the medium HR September 6th, 2001 in "Judas' experiences of the Hells."

What really happens after death?

helping others. One needs to repent, in the sense of accepting responsibility for where you are, and wanting to change. But most of all one needs to learn to be more loving. This as one can expect, is not easy. Particularly when those around you are not loving. While saying that this is the category of help you might get, if it was a Catholic priest offering help you might expect him to suggest you follow his faith. The extent to which this sort of narrow religious advice is given, really depends on the level of advancement of the spirit offering the advice. The more advanced spirits do realize that many conventional religions have much the same effect, and that therefore love is the common denominator. But lower down most spirits cling tenaciously to their religious beliefs. So you may get a lot of pastors all favouring their brand of religion, trying to help you. But there are also many organized groups of people who do not ascribe to any specific religious belief who offer help to those in the dark planes. They typically have names like: "The Brotherhood of Hope".

The reason why this process is so slow is that we are as we think. Amazingly, thoughts have been described as real, and as having a real existence in this realm. We have to change our thoughts in order to change, and that can be hard.

The second category of advice that you might receive introduces a totally new concept. Here you will be told that if you pray from the heart (soul) to God and ask for His Divine Love, you will feel this Love. It may take a few days, or a week, but you will feel this Love as a real sensation. If you keep on asking, each time you will receive a small portion of Divine Love. This Love is a physical reality, and will purify your soul. This is the short cut method. Not only does it get you out of darkness faster than any other way, but also it will accelerate your spiritual progress through the heavens. Many dark spirits have attested to its effectiveness, but they also caution how hard it is to think of spiritual things while in hell. Of course since almost nobody has heard of this short cut method, they may dismiss it out of hand. But since it promises almost instant results, I suggest it is well worth trying. You don't have anything to lose.

This technique also works on earth. That is to say, you can feel the Love, and you will notice yourself changing over the next year or so. And we have had confirmation that humans following this method are in general much brighter in their spirit body than the general mortal population. It does something at a very fundamental level.

The First Sphere.

Hell is of course in the first sphere, but most of us would not consider the upper reaches of the First Sphere as being in darkness. That is because we are used to earth, a planet that is itself largely in darkness. Above "hell" one finds the "Twilight Zone", and then "Summerland". These are spiritualist terms. Some spiritualists teach that Summerland is the Third Sphere, but that is apparently not so, they are simply numbering sub-spheres as major spheres.

In the upper reaches of the first sphere spirits use tools to create things, just like here. Later on, this is unnecessary because they learn how to use their minds instead. They live in homes, and learn how to manipulate their spirit bodies. They can for example have a perfect physique, or a full head of hair. Most spirits choose a physical form from somewhere between twenty and thirty, one which I guess represents their physical prime.

Here the spirits find that their desires result in changes to their spirit bodies. So, although they do not initially have conscious control over this aspect, they do look attractive, with perfect bodies. In time these "material" pleasures pall, and the spirit finds itself drawn more to spiritual avenues, and that this gives it increased happiness. At that stage they are then starting to progress out of this sphere.

They also discover making love in the spirit is a bit different and very enjoyable. It is accomplished by a sort of fusion of energy between the souls. Having been fortunate enough to experience it a few times in out of body experiences, I can report that it is indeed something to look forward to. Homes are provided too. The way in which buildings and other created items are made is intriguing, and explained by Monsignor Robert Hugh Benson[123]. Apparently you can decorate or change your home. Folks specialize in all these activities, including for example making flowers. The flowers are eternal in nature, and responsive. I rather suspect we will not have an autumn in heaven, and that slightly saddens me. There is no decay, so I can't see how one achieves the magic show of autumn leaves that we have here on earth.

---

[123] *"Life in the World Unseen"* by Anthony Borgia.

Is Reincarnation an Illusion?

Of course one could create an unchanging autumn show, but that would not be quite the same.

Even the homes in the upper planes of the First Sphere are very comfortable, allowing for the fact that they don't have kitchens or bathrooms, but later on they seem to be better than the grandest mansion one might imagine. In hell they are hovels or caves, although apparently many cities also exist there. The old Bible phrase – "in my Father's house are many mansions" has more than a ring of Truth. But the weather is so benevolent, that if you did not want to live in a house, you could entirely do without one.

Animals and pets are found in spirit. There is no doubt at all if you have a much loved cat, dog or even elephant, that you will enjoy its companionship again. It is not the case that all animals automatically survive death, but much loved ones are found again. It is likely that this is a creation emanating from the love that we hold for that animal. On the other hand, apparently there are places in the spirit world where you can go and see the dinosaurs, so no doubt all manner of animal can be found, for our enjoyment. Of course many pets pass over before us, and thus someone will be looking after them there.

Strangely many spirits report feeling cold when they first arrive, but later this is not a problem. It is quite widely accepted that spirits are cold when they appear in our realm, and at least one spirit has reported being able to feel the heat from a fire in our realm, as well as clearly hearing sound from our realm.

Spirits spend a great deal of time discussing God. Does He exist etc. Naturally religious groups exist, and spirits will follow those beliefs by attending church etc. Spiritual ignorance abounds, as one would expect. That does not mean spirits are un-opinionated. Indeed it seems some of the most opinionated spirits can be found in the First and Second Spheres. The old adage of the empty can making the most noise seems true of spirit as well. Arguments are even more intense than on earth. This is because each spirit will now have some experiences that support their belief.

The level of ignorance is actually very high, but that does not stop many spirits attending séances and coming through with a great deal of misplaced authority. These are the spirits who may use Jesus' name, or even call themselves God. One also finds spirits here who are mischievous, and immature, rather than evil. They will also delight in frightening mortals at séances.

Summerland has been described as having a climate similar to California. But without the pollution! There are a great number of children in Summerland, but they are not found lower, which is quite reasonable. The landscape is beautiful, with pretty villages and cities. Spirits can choose to live in a city, or in the country. The cities don't have roads, indeed there are no roads anywhere, and typically the height of the buildings is limited to a few stories. So the typical landscape of a city would be quite different to what we might be used to, with no pavements or tables on sidewalks. But the grander buildings have large paved areas, and patio areas.

There is still a degree of negativity, which is illustrated by gossip, differences of opinion, and anger. But most spirits are pretty used to that from earth, and probably don't really notice it. Sports are indulged, but there are issues playing ball sports. Apparently the gravity is quite different, and to launch a ball one needs to use thought power. Once so launched, it will not stop until redirected again by thought. So sending a ball towards the goal would always reach the goal, and rather seems to make sports such as football and golf irrelevant. That might hugely upset some folks, so I hope there is something as addictive for the golfing fraternity. I was very pleased to discover one can have a boat, if one has the development, and that this can be "motorised" by thought. It is even possible to sail, but as the winds are very gentle, I guess it is again largely thought powered.

It is here in the First Sphere that spirits tend to discover what they really want to do, and what talents they have. As they don't have to work, and there is no authority chasing them, they are totally free to devote whatever time they like to pursuits. Spirits find that they can follow material pursuits here, but in time the attractiveness of that fades, and suddenly they begin to realize that spirituality is important, and a greater source of happiness.

The Second Sphere.

The essential requirement for a spirit to reach the Second Sphere is the recognition that material pursuits are limited, and do not lead to real happiness. In the second sphere, spirits choose their spiritual path. These are by no means uniform, and in general, if a spirit decides later to change to another spiritual path, they will return to this sphere.

In fact there are two great classifications of spiritual path, but this distinction is probably not obvious to most spirits. The first classification is the Natural Love path. In this class, one finds all the religions, and even those following an intellectual, and non-religious path. Many people have remarked that love is the basis of most religions, but the love they are referring to is the Natural love. Slowly but surely, spirits become more loving, and advance steadily through the spheres, stopping at the sixth, but generally bypassing the Third and Fifth. The Sixth is a heaven of complete happiness, so complete that spirits lack nothing, and cannot envisage anything better.

The second classification is the Divine Love path. If you took the short cut out of hell, you will have found so much happiness flowing into your soul that this will be the path you will follow. Not many spirits follow this path however.

In this Second Sphere, which can be called a sphere of decision, it is really like a kindergarten. In the first spheres, many things were built by machine. Here in the second, spirits are learning to use their spirit powers, assisted by other more advanced spirits. There are many institutions of learning, and this sphere is well known to many spiritualists.

They learn to modify their clothes, to build their houses using spiritual power, and to even modify aspects of their spiritual bodies. This exposure to the spiritual powers that are available generates a state of euphoria, and as a result many spirits stay here a long time. It is such fun. That is no bad thing; there is no timetable to keep.

What really happens after death?

In deciding what development path to follow, spirits are influenced by those from more advanced spheres. Thus a spirit from the Fourth Sphere may well extol the virtues of his path, and the beauty of his sphere. Spirits in many cases retain some of the spiritual ideas they had in the first sphere, but they may be beginning to modify those to some extent. Some of them have a period of confusion, for example if they believe that they should now stand before God, or perhaps Jesus. As that does not happen, it takes a while to rationalize, and evolve a new spiritual or religious strategy.

Jesus does visit these spirits, but they do not generally recognize him. He cannot display himself as he really is because his spiritual brightness is far too powerful to be revealed in these lower spheres, and hence they generally do not accord him any special status. We have been told that the sun is like a candle compared to his spiritual brightness. All more advanced spirits have to limit the brightness they display in the lower levels.

The Second Sphere is a real heaven, as it has immense facilities for study, facilities that cannot be dreamed of on earth. Eventually however, each and every spirit eventually arrives at the highest plane in this sphere. There a tremendous change occurs. They remember that they have got this far through the help given them by numerous spirits, and a great urge overtakes them to perform a similar function. It is an atonement task.

The Third Sphere.

Spirits in the Third Sphere have both sufficient love, and spiritual understanding to begin to perform a useful task of helping other spirits. Because of their greater spiritual development, they can also begin to perceive the Will of God, although this is not because they can perceive God.

Typically the tasks that they undertake have something to do with their earth life. I came across a fellow getting a lot of help from an ex-playgirl. This fellow had very strong sexual desires, and she was trying very hard to influence him away from those. Clearly she had to atone for inciting so many fellows to sexual desires by being a playgirl. Another may be a pastor, who has spent a lifetime spreading false doctrines. He may find himself trying to undo those false beliefs. This work can be very hard, and these spirits do experience frustration. However this does not mean that all these spirits are teaching only truth. These spirits still have many of their earth beliefs, provided always that none of these are seriously harmful from a spiritual perspective. Where that is the case, they do not progress until they come to a realisation that their belief is false.

Those spirits following the Divine Love path may spend a long time in this sphere, because they feel the importance of the task of teaching this "new" Truth. As they also do not find the Fourth Sphere particularly congenial, they would generally stay here till they can reach the Fifth. When finally what started out as a work of atonement, and now becomes a vocational choice, the spirit is ready to move on. Here is a description of a home in the Third Sphere:

> *Yes, my home is very beautiful and I am perfectly delighted with it. It is made of white marble and is surrounded by lawns and flowers and trees of various kinds. The grass is so very green and the flowers are so beautiful and variegated. The trees are always in foliage and have such beautiful limbs and leaves. I am most pleased with my home, I mean the building. There are many beautiful pictures on the walls, and the walls are all frescoed and hung with fine coverings, and the floors are inlaid with beautiful mosaics. I have all the splendid*

furniture that I could possibly wish for, and my library is full of books of all kinds, especially of those that tell of God and His Love for man. You would be in your element if you could be with me.

I have music, such as you never heard on earth, and instruments of various kinds which I am learning to play, and I sing with all my heart and soul as the days go by. I have beds on which I lie down, but I never sleep. We do not need sleep here; we only rest, for sometimes we get tired from our work and are greatly refreshed by lying on the beds and couches which are so comfortable that we do not realize that we are tired after lying down a little while.[124]

---

[124] https://new-birth.net/link22/ received by James Padgett on November 30th, 1914

Is Reincarnation an Illusion?

The Fourth Sphere.

The spirits in this sphere are now used as teachers in the various learning institutions, and they develop in this sphere their sometimes astonishing healing abilities. It is largely an intellectual sphere, and some spirits following a Divine Love path spend almost no time here, moving virtually directly on to the Fifth Sphere once they are able. Others chose to stay here, although they can do much the same work in the Fifth Sphere. There is beginning to be a bigger and bigger difference between spirits following the Natural Love and the intellectual path, and those following the Divine Love path.

Earthly bonds weaken, and spirits are not much interested in the affairs of earth. Even familial bonds weaken. This does not mean that they do not care for other members of their genetic families, but their general love for all mankind is now so strong, that familial love recedes in contrast.

Soul mates now begin to be a topic of great interest. It is true we all have a soul mate.[125] This is because the initial creation of souls creates pairs of souls. This appears to be yet another technique that God has provided to gather his creation closer. Inevitably one soul mate will be more advanced. Their great love for each other spurs the less developed one to make great efforts to catch up, so that they can live together. Sometimes this is in fact the way a soul is "extracted" from the hells. The more advanced soul mate is able to influence the less developed one to make the effort to get out of darkness. What is intriguing is that this soul mate attraction is so strong that a bright and pure spirit is actually attracted at all to a dark spirit.

The Fourth Sphere, with its great facilities is often a sphere where spirits stay a very long time. By the time that these spirits have reached the upper planes of this sphere, they will have all but lost interest in the affairs of mortal man. Their only interest is in helping man to progress, but they take no personal interest in his affairs.

---

[125] See https://new-birth.net/link23/

The Fifth Sphere.

This is what is termed a soul sphere and those spirits following a Natural Love path do not spend much time here. But it is an important sphere for Divine Love spirits. The only thing that Natural Love spirits lack is absolute purity. They must eradicate the last traces of sin. They may still cling to false beliefs, but none of these will be harmful. This last stage of purification does not take long and the Natural Love spirits then progress into the sixth, the ultimate goal of their spiritual path.

There is no reason for them to tarry here since there is more happiness to be had in the sixth. There is also little commonality between them and Divine love spirits. They have fundamentally different beliefs and spiritual path, and this leads to different interests.

In fact many of the Divine Love spirits also hasten to enter the sixth, and then return. The sixth is not entirely congenial to them and they have much development that they can do in the Fifth. And once they have received more of the Divine Love, they can progress directly to the Seventh Sphere.

It was reported that Mother Teresa passed over into the Fifth Sphere and that is the highest that we have heard of for a mortal, although there have been others. Just recently we heard that Francis of Assisi also passed into the Fifth as did a long-time follower of the Padgett Messages – Dr. Leslie Stone.[126] Few could doubt the love that Mother Teresa had, or the spiritual fervour that Francis of Assisi had. What is interesting is neither Mother Teresa nor Francis of Assisi would have been schooled in the concept of Divine Love, yet their spiritual fervour was such that they followed this path automatically. It is in fact possible to find this path intuitively and it is probably something that has distinguished many of the "saints".

Here is a description of a home in the Fifth Sphere:

---

[126] Dr. Leslie Stone was the original publisher of the Padgett Messages under the title *"True Gospel Revealed Anew by Jesus."* See this message: https://new-birth.net/link24/

Is Reincarnation an Illusion?

> *I am living with your mother in her home, but I am not so spiritual as she. We are both very happy though, and have everything that the heart could wish for. The music is so beautiful that I cannot describe it to you, and even the love which helps to make the music is of such an intensity that you could not possibly understand if I should attempt to tell it to you. My home here is much more beautiful than that which I had in the third sphere, and everything is beyond what I conceived when I lived there. The house and trees and flowers and fruits are very much more beautiful and delightful.*
>
> *No one could be anything but happy in such a home. We have nothing to interfere with our happiness and every one is a delightful companion and full of love and beauty. I have met many spirits that I did not know either on earth or in the spirit world before I came to this place, both men and women.*
>
> *Yes, we have rivers and lakes and fields and mountains and all the beautiful landscapes that you can imagine, I not only enjoy these things, but they are more real than those of earth. I am sometimes engaged in painting these flowers and landscapes, and have many pictures which others painted. I find that I can paint with a more artistic touch than when on earth. I have no trouble in drawing as you know I had some in my earth pictures. I am also studying music, and especially my vocal lessons. You will be much surprised when you hear me sing as you cannot conceive what a different voice I have. Sometimes I try to sing some of the songs that I used to sing to you, but they are not pretty in comparison to the songs we have here, either in the music or the sentiments.*[127]

---

[127] https://new-birth.net/link25/ received by James Padgett on January 7th 1915

The Sixth Sphere.

This is the pinnacle of spiritual development for Natural Love spirits. It represents a return to the Adamic state. However they quite possibly would dispute that there are any higher spheres. Certainly Divine Love spirits find that these spirits are not interested in listening to this concept. They enjoy themselves with many very advanced intellectual and moral discussions. One should realize that mental capacity has expanded enormously along with spiritual development. This is a perfect heaven and spirits lack for nothing, and cannot imagine that anything better could exist.

The Sixth Sphere is a purely intellectual area and by that I mean that in spite of the great spirituality of the place, the zeal of its inhabitants goes much more for increasing their knowledge, while they live a life in absolute harmony with God's laws of spirituality. It is a place where science has reached its most spectacular results compared to all the spiritual spheres and where the intelligence of its inhabitants is supreme, and where absolute fraternity exists, such as people dream of on earth. There are great social events, amusements, all of which provides them with great happiness, their class of happiness. Paradise, yes, the Sixth Sphere is the Paradise which the Hebrews dreamt of and continue dreaming of, and it is the Paradise that Christian churches teach of and also spiritualists.

Religion is important too and there is a great diversity of religious practice. That indicates that the inhabitants are not in possession of absolute truth. It is rare for these spirits to communicate with mortals. But many work as teachers and professors in lower spheres.

Divine Love spirits can enter this sphere, but generally do not stay long. They simply find that their interests are different. So they return to the Fifth until they are able to pass into the Seventh.

As these Sixth Sphere spirits do not progress any further, it is not known what their long-term future will be. Some sources suggest eventually all will awaken to the fact that something is lacking – God's Divine Love and progress will then resume. Other sources suggest that in fact the "second death" will mean that these spirits are isolated and the "gates" to the Kingdom of God will be closed, leaving them

Is Reincarnation an Illusion?

excluded. Another revelation[128] suggests their future will lie in the local universe in which the earth lies, rather than being able to reach other parts of this universe, or the Central Paradise where Father resides, or even other universes.

---

[128] *The Urantia Book*

The Seventh Sphere.

This sphere is only populated by Divine Love spirits. It marks the beginning of a series of changes that will eventually leave them quite different to other spirits. So different, that it is said they cannot be considered to be of the same family. The first change is that the soul manifests a mind, which is different to the material mind that all other spirits utilize. This begins to dominate. Eventually, before the spirit leaves this sphere, the material mind of the spirit body will have entirely withered away, leaving the spirit using the mind of the soul. (There is a different perspective on this, that rather than "growing" a soul mind we actually start to access the Divine mind of our Indwelling Spirit.)

The duration of the process of the last stage of transformation varies. It may be achieved in a relatively short time, but many spirits stay longer in this wonderful paradise, enjoying and experiencing, like tourists taking their time to explore the last corner of their unknown world.

They gain enormous knowledge in this sphere, in this process and without study. The knowledge simply comes to them. Eventually they are ready for the transition. In the transition to the Celestial heavens which lie above the Seventh Sphere, they fuse with their Indwelling Spirit, or Thought Adjuster[129] which has accompanied them since their earliest years. This gives the Indwelling Spirit personality and the spirit gains Divinity and immortality. Spirits who have passed this stage tell us they know they are immortal. There is no debate, such as exists in the Sixth Sphere. They then become spiritual beings, as opposed to semi-material beings. This difference must be subtle because other less developed spirits do not seem able to discern the difference. Or perhaps it's simply the fact that when an advanced spirit visits lower spheres, they find that they take on more of the "hues" of those levels and thus the difference is not great at that level.

There are "un-numbered" spheres in the Celestial Heavens above, each more magnificent than the rest. Spirits who reside here complain that words simply cannot describe these spheres and generally they

---

[129] The name used in *The Urantia Book*.

Is Reincarnation an Illusion?

just won't try. These would appear to be the classic **Kingdom of God** that the Christian Bible talks about. But this concludes our summary. Ironically, because this is probably only the start of our next adventure, the re-birth by spirit that the Christian Bible promises to those who have faith that Father loves us. And an eternity of growth and spiritual adventure lies ahead. Perhaps there will be another narrow path we might have to navigate beyond the Kingdom of God? A particularly good video of this long journey to Paradise, based on the Urantia book, can be found on this web site: http://www.squarecircles.com/

Recommended reading:

"True Gospel Revealed Anew by Jesus", Volumes I to IV. (The Padgett Messages)
"Life in the World Unseen", by Anthony Borgia
"More About Life in the World Unseen" by Anthony Borgia
"Here and Hereafter" by Anthony Borgia
"Through the Mists" by Robert James Lees
"The Life Elysian" by Robert James Lees
"The Gate of Heaven" by Robert James Lees
"Spirit World and Spirit Life" by Charlotte Elizabeth Dresser
"Life Here and Hereafter" by Charlotte Elizabeth Dresser
"The Blue Island" by Pardoe Woodman and Estelle Stead
"30 Years among the Dead" by Dr Carl Wickland
"Remote Depossession" by Dr. Irene Hickman.[130]
"A Wanderer in the Spirit Lands" by Franchezzo.
"Gone West" by J.S.M Ward
"Letters from the Light" by Elsa Barker
"The Urantia Book" published by the Urantia Foundation.
"Love Without End" by Glenda Green.
"When Ghosts Speak" by Mary Ann Winkowski.
"Entangled Minds" by Dean Radin.
"The Law of Attraction" by Esther and Jerry Hicks.
"Life on the Other Side" by Silvia Browne.
"Cosmic Voyage" by Courtney Browne, Ph.D.
"Astral Travel" by Gavin and Yvonne Frost.
"A Subaltern in Spirit Land – a sequel to Gone West Part One" by J.S.M. Ward
"Where God Lives" by Melvin Morse, M.D.
"More Alive Than Ever"...Always Karen by Jeanne Walker.[131]
Five Volumes of "The Life Beyond the Veil" by Rev. George Vale Owen.

---

[130] Contact details for the publisher of this book, and where new copies can be purchased, are: Hickman Healing Foundation, P.O. Box 42, Knoxville, IA 50138. They also have a website at http://hickman-healing-foundation.org

[131] This book and its first publication as "Always Karen" are hard to find, but I have created a Kindle version. See https://new-birth.net/link8/

Printed in Great Britain
by Amazon